APORE    TOKYO

the British Library on request.

Heinemann Educational
A division of Heinemann Publishers (Oxford) Ltd
Halley Court, Jordan Hill, Oxford OX2 8EJ

OXFORD LONDON EDINBURGH
MADRID ATHENS BOLOGNA PARIS
MELBOURNE SYDNEY AUCKLAND SING
IBADAN NAIROBI HARARE GABORONE
PORTSMOUTH NH (USA)

First published 1992

92 93 94 95 96 10 9 8 7 6 5 4 3 2 1

A catalogue record for this book is available from

ISBN 0 435 800426

Typeset by Taurus Graphics, Kidlington, Oxon
Printed in great Britain by Clays Ltd, St. Ives plc

# Contents

## SECTION D
# Instruments

# Introduction

## A1
## Managing a better school

### ■ What is the purpose of the book?

This book has been written to help those who manage schools, for three reasons:

1  **The increased powers delegated to heads and governors make them more accountable.**

   Their decisions and the school's 'performance' are open to much increased public scrutiny. They therefore need a means of investigating what goes on in their schools, of justifying it, and of securing improvement where necessary.

2  **School development needs to be 'owned' by the school community.**

   Education has for some years been 'initiative driven'. GCSE, TVEI, National Curriculum and appraisal are just some of the major developments to which schools have had to adapt. These initiatives have arrived piecemeal. In order to sustain motivation, teachers need to be able to answer 'yes' to two questions:

   • Is there coherence in all initiatives? It could be a jigsaw puzzle in which all the pieces fit together to make a pleasing picture, or a firework display, in which a number of attractive but separate items blaze briefly and separately across the sky.

   • Can we make the developments ours? If not, are they merely someone else's agenda?

   If the answers are 'no', then schools and their teachers are being buffeted by one juggernaut after another. This book stresses coherence by bringing initiatives together in a way which, following from point 1, is locally managed and owned.

3   **There is a need to bring research on effective schools into contact with the day-to-day issues facing those schools.**

There is abundant research on the 'school effect', and upon the 'effective school'; there are well-tried and tested instruments to enquire into the behaviour and performance of organisations; there is a common agenda of issues in most schools. The three are here brought together to help managers improve their schools for the benefit of the communities they serve, especially the students and their parents.

## ▉ What is in this book?

This is a practical working manual to help school managers – especially senior staff, but also governors – respond positively to their delegated responsibilities by **managing for quality**.

The book is based around a set of key ideas:

1   Ensuring improvement in performance is the central task of senior management.

2   Staff and other partners in the school must be involved and committed – quality is *everybody's* job.

3   95% of what a school does is to maintain, and only the remaining 5% can be called development; but that 'improvement' applies to both.

4   After the business of teaching its students, the organisation has little residual time or energy; these precious resources must be focused, not dissipated.

5   The amount of genuine development work which can be properly managed is therefore limited.

6   The 'reflective professional' approach – by individual or institution – leads most effectively to improvement, but a critical outside view is necessary.

7   The plans and data which these processes produce, as well as serving the prime need of school improvement, may also fulfil accountability requirements to governors, parents, LEA, in a way which involves them.

After this Introduction (A), which helps the user through the book and examines the concept of 'quality' used in it, the three main sections are:

## B   BUILDING IN QUALITY

This presents research data on school effectiveness, with detailed consideration of each of the component parts of the review and development cycle.

## C   IMPROVING PERFORMANCE

This contains case studies based on familiar situations in school; the studies generally consist of a context, a suggested investigation to collect and examine data using instruments from (D), and follow-up action.

## D   INSTRUMENTS

This section offers a number of tools to gather and handle data, with guidance on their use.

There are copious cross-references, especially between Sections B and C. Because this is a working document for busy people and not a textbook, there is little extended prose – more material is presented in the form of numbered lists, bullet points, diagrams and grids.

We have tried to:

- reject slick answers; there is no magic wand nor a single approach which makes it all easy;

- avoid needless jargon;

- use a case study and workshop approach, in the form of questions or investigations which are real, live concerns for schools;

- use a succinct approach, attempting one page plans wherever possible;

- get behind phrases which trip lightly off the tongue – 'supported self-evaluation', 'target-setting', 'priority-setting', 'audit' – to help clarify the 'what and how';

- present practical ideas in a clear way, but one which promotes the creativity of the reader to use and develop, or reject and replace, our ideas.

## ◼   How to use the book

Readers can gain access to the book in three main ways:

1   A desire to look at some of the basics in the school – what makes a good school, the role of the school development plan or the part played by external inspection – leads into the sub-sections of B.

2   A school confronted by an issue – such as a priority in the school development plan, a problem such as a poor set of GCSE results, or a forthcoming in-service day – may relate quickly to the case studies around real issues which make up the sub-sections of C.

3   The school which is undertaking an investigation of an aspect of its performance may look first at the suggested instruments in D.

In each case, the abundant cross-references should help the reader move around the book – and indeed can stimulate the making of hitherto-ignored connections.

## ■ For whom is it written?

The manual is targeted primarily at those who manage or aspire to manage secondary schools – senior staff and governors. It may be useful to think in terms of the following matrix (fig 1), which intersects possible users with possible needs; a few examples have been given.

| USERS | OBJECTIVES | | | |
| | Policy development | Curriculum development | Staff development | Personal development |
|---|---|---|---|---|
| Senior Management Team | as a source of prompts and checklists for action | | | |
| Governors | | | use of case studies as governor training materials | |
| Middle Managers | | | | to help career development towards deputyship |
| Staff | | use of data collection techniques to enhance classroom research & self-appraisal | | |

Figure 1   Users of *Managing a Better School*

# A2
# Quality in education

When we use the term 'quality', or talk of 'improving performance', we take this to mean:

- **efficiency** – that what the school says in its aims and in the priorities listed in its development plan are in fact carried out;

- **effectiveness** – that the school satisfies external criteria, such as the demands of parents and students, and does well against comparable institutions in key areas of performance such as examination results.

Process and product are not in opposition in our model. Schools exist to bring benefit to young people; in order to be deemed 'good', a school must stand up to scrutiny. The available evidence supports the view that schools which operate in particular ways, such as in a culture of self-evaluation involving all staff, in the context of a school development plan which focuses the energies of the school community on a number of rationally-derived priorities, are best-placed to fulfil their objectives and achieve the best for their students.

The diagram (fig 2), together with section A3 (*Abbeydown School: Policy for self-evaluation*), summarises our model of quality. The main proposals are: that the **improvement of quality** is everyone's job, led by the SMT and governors; that the **development of quality** is a continuous process, based on a well-managed regime of review and development which links four components:

1   An **internal cycle of self-evaluation** (A3) based around the **school development plan** (B2,3). The planning sets priorities or targets (B7), each of which has built-in success criteria (B7), to enable progress checking. There is an annual review meeting (B6) at which the process is 'freeze-framed' and new targets set.

2   **Data on performance** (B5) in key areas, to enable comparison through time for one school, and between schools which can reasonably be compared.

3   **Feedback** from all those who are involved in the school on how they think it is doing, and what should be done – students, staff, parents, governors, business community (B8).

**4**   **External inspection** (B9) on a regular basis, to add objectivity – or at least the subjectivity of experienced outsiders.

Of these four components the first has supremacy. This is for two reasons:

- Evaluation of learning is a sophisticated business – although classrooms may be checked and impressions given during a brief inspection, a thorough investigation involves looking at a lot of children over a long period of time to evaluate their achievement. Such longitudinal studies are only possible by the institution itself.

- If change is to result from the process of evaluation, then the process and the results of that evaluation must belong to the school, its head, staff and governors. Without such ownership, it is probable that critical comment will produce a defensive reaction and that the comment will be marginalised.

Figure 2 shows how the other three components feed data into the basic school 'quality cycle', and improve the basis upon which planning takes place.

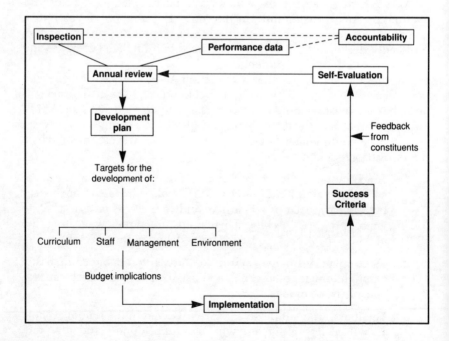

Figure 2    A quality cycle for use in schools

# A3
# Abbeydown School: policy for self-evaluation

Throughout the book, reference will be made to this imaginary school. The case study materials deliberately do not involve detailed knowledge of the school, since this tends to lead to unhelpful concentration on the **differences** between institutions, rather than on their **common features**, which is what we want to stress. Suffice to say that we have envisaged Abbeydown as a medium-sized 11–18 school, with a senior management team of headteacher, two deputies and one incentive allowance E postholder. The school is organised around four large faculties, and has a pastoral system based on years.

When the new headteacher came to Abbeydown, she had a particular philosophy of school development. It seemed to the staff to be based on two principles:

- the involvement of staff and other constituents: governors, parents, the community, students;

- a measured pace and an approach which stressed coherence – a single plan for development which took in a number of potentially separate elements, such as budget, inspection reports and departmental plans for the National Curriculum.

This was welcomed, but at an early staff meeting the head was asked to explain her approach and justify it. This, the resulting paper, was drafted by the senior management team, underwent discussion in various groups of staff and governors, and was eventually published in the staff handbook.

1   Why self-evaluation?

- we have been 'initiative-driven' for years (GCSE, TVEI, NC etc.) In order that we can 'own' the changes we enact, we need to move towards an 'institution-driven' form of development;
- to acknowledge the local management culture – we not only make the decisions, we have to stand up and justify them, and be accountable for the results; therefore we need to know how we are doing;
- to make the school development plan a 'live' document;
- thereby to give staff and governors ownership of the development of the school;

and above all

- **to improve the school still further for the benefit of the students in it and to come; and for their parents**.

2   The role of the school development plan

One main purpose of the school development plan is to control the pace of development, keeping it as far as possible manageable by identifying a 'do-able' number of priorities in a rational and open way, and then communicating them to those who are associated with the school – including the students. The themes for self-evaluation are therefore the priorities in the plan. The timescale of the plan is approximately three years and it is reviewed annually.

3   The role of the Annual Review

Just as the school development plan is a summative statement in the development process, so the Annual Review is a 'freeze-frame' in the self-evaluation process. Once a year, normally in November, we bring together the key people in executing the priorities in the school develop-ment plan, to check progress against targets, consider the client feed-back and school performance data, set new targets, and commission new investigations from within the school, from the LEA and from other consultants. At the staff meeting following the review, the outcomes will be discussed and working groups set up (see 5 below).

4   Themes for self-evaluation

The annual programme will consist of:

- cyclic review: each year we will review the work of three curricular areas, one year group and one cross/whole-curricular theme; this means that we will evaluate the major work of the school on an approxi-mate five-year cycle;
- an annual look at basic performance indication [B5], which may create priorities for investigation;
- a survey of the views of parents, governors, students etc of aspects on current interest [B8];
- the priority themes of the school development plan [B2,3,7].

These will not necessarily be treated as separate investigations; we should seek overlap and convergence.

5   Involvement of staff

- Cyclic reviews will be managed by the member of the senior management team with responsibility, together with the head of year/section/department/coordinator. 'Named' governors will be involved where possible.

- Whole-school reviews based on school development plan priorities, on client or performance indicator data, will be carried out by small groups (maximum six) of staff, with non-teaching staff, parents and governors involved where possible and appropriate. Teaching staff will normally be from departments not part of the cyclic review in that year, and will be volunteers. Groups will be set up at or following the staff meeting after the annual review (see 3).

- It is expected that all staff would be involved in such a review team about once in every three years.

Headteacher

# Building in quality

## B1
## What makes a good school?

### Introduction

The years since the early 1980s have been the decades of educational accountability. Schools have been called to account for themselves in ways which were never heard of in earlier decades. The competitive climate which allows the 'good schools' to flourish whilst the 'bad schools' go into terminal decline has encouraged a simplistic way of measuring a school's qualities.

Publication of examination results has led to the production of league tables which seek to use spurious measures to compare vastly different schools. Thus, a *Sunday Times* report: '250 of the best', sought to rank schools according to the percentage of sixth formers gaining A or B grades at 'A' level. Such a measure pays no heed to the 'good' schools that have no sixth form; neither does it allow for the success of those schools which cater for students of lower ability. More seriously, though, it seeks to measure a school according to only one of its outcomes; albeit, some might say, the most important one.

Measures of outcome are, clearly, the most clear-cut indicators of a school's achievement. Examination results, attendance rates and staying-on rates provide straightforward measures of performance. Such data may be used to inform discussions about a school's outcome efficiency when seen in the context of other relevant information germane to the school, its locale and intake. However, such data do not provide truth about how 'good' a school is; rather, they can be used to inform review and help set targets for school improvement (see Section B5).

More important than the simplistic data of input-output, which seek to equate schools with the manufacturing industry, are the more subtle and elusive aspects of the process of education which make certain schools effective and others less so. International research into school effectiveness emanated from the United States in the 1970s and has subsequently developed in the United Kingdom as well as in Australasia, Canada and Scandinavia. In the United Kingdom, the work of Reynolds and Rutter is of particular significance.

According to the school effectiveness researchers, there are certain common factors which are characteristic of the 'good' school; that is to say, the school which achieves academic success for its students once home background and ability factors have been taken into account. A summary of these factors follows.

## ■ Teaching in the effective school

- The school has a set of commonly-held aims which are understood by teachers and students. These collective values are founded upon the belief that all individuals are worthy of respect and have a contribution to make to the school.

- An atmosphere of mutual trust and respect is fostered through open communication by teachers and students.

- Teachers have a commitment to learning and a belief that all students are able to achieve. The headteacher, teachers and students have high expectations of achievement and make few excuses for under-performance.

- There is good discipline in the school, achieved through the maintenance of safe and sensible rules.

- The environment is kept in a good state of repair and is respected by the students.

- A high proportion of lesson time is spent upon teaching and learning; a purposeful pace is maintained. Little time is spent on disciplinary matters or lesson preparation during lesson time. Lessons begin and end on time.

- The teacher employs a range of approaches within a lesson or sequence of lessons. The teacher deploys him/herself to the class as a whole, to groups and to individuals in order to modulate the lesson's pace and rigour.

- The teacher values students' contributions and makes use of praise and reward to underline the value of achievement and the pursuit of excellence.

- Students receive clear feedback on their performance and are shown what is expected of them. Assessment is regular, formative and diagnostic.

- Teachers regularly set, monitor and mark homework.

- The curriculum is seen to be relevant to students' immediate and long-term needs.

# ■ Leadership in the effective school

- The headteacher places great emphasis upon the quality of the classroom experience. He/she is aware of what is happening in classrooms and spends a considerable amount of time observing teaching. Students are aware of the headteacher's involvement in the day-to-day life of the school.

- The headteacher is aware of teachers' needs, offers feedback in response to performance, makes use of praise, encourages teachers' long-term professional development and uses that development for the good of the school.

- The headteacher delegates responsibility and trusts colleagues to perform efficiently.

- The headteacher manages the school consistently, fairly but flexibly. Resources are allocated as a consequence of review and needs analysis for the good of the students' learning.

- The headteacher provides positive leadership; he/she sets goals and motivates the staff to be committed to their achievement.

- The headteacher is willing to take risks; teachers trust him/her to know what he/she is doing since there is an agreement that all should be for the good of the students.

# ■ Management towards school effectiveness

David Reynolds in 'Managing for Improved School Effectiveness: An International Survey' (*School Organisation* Vol 9 No 2) itemises certain principles which underlie the management of increased school effectiveness. The key factors may be summarised as follows:

- School improvement programmes should be school-based, school-focused and whole-school in their orientation.

- School change should make use of external support by way of consultative assistance and advice.

- Change should not merely be a matter of structural or organisational change; it should take into account staff relationships, feelings and attitudes.

- Change should follow a school-based review or appraisal so that the need for development has been identified through objective data.

- Organisational change needs to be wedded to curriculum and methodological development if it is to win the hearts and minds of teachers.

- The change process should be long-term and concerned with a cycle of **review** ⇒ **improvement** ⇒ **evaluation** ⇒ **further improvement**.

## ◼ Summary

1    The 'good' school has a clear vision and purpose which is understood by all parties, including parents.

2    The 'good' school believes in a collective and collegial approach to relationships, management, decision-making and planning.

3    The 'good' school has a well-established cycle of review and development aimed at the effective use of resources for the benefit of students' learning.

4    The 'good' school values quality in teaching and learning; it has high expectations and encourages achievement and success.

# B2
# Assembling the school development plan

## ◼ Introduction

It is clear from the work of Reynolds and others (see Section B1) that the 'good' school is managed through a school development plan which enables all members of staff to have a coherent view of the direction and priorities to be taken for school improvement.

The DFE, LEAs and others have provided school managers with guidance towards this end in recent years. Caldwell and Spinks' book *The Self-managing school* describes the experience of Australian schools who took the way of greater autonomy earlier than other western educational systems. In the United Kingdom, the DFE 'School Development Planning Project' group, chaired by David Hargreaves, provided guidance for schools and LEAs during the early 1990s.

As a result, most school managers have embarked upon an approach to school development planning with the aim of responding positively to the changing educational world for the benefit of their students and teachers. Although coherence is the central principle of development planning, few plans have achieved this end. For some teachers, the school development plan is a paperwork exercise which has little impact upon their working practices.

# ■ Coherent Planning

In some schools, the development plan has emerged as a consequence of soul-searching by the headteacher or senior management team. Such a document may serve to prioritise action for the school's managers but does not ensure coherent involvement by all members of the teaching and non-teaching staff. As has been observed in Section B1, the 'good' school believes in a collective and collegial approach to management, decision making and planning. This approach requires consultation and time in order to ensure the full involvement and commitment of staff. Above all, the development plan worth having needs to fit into a review cycle which enables all involved to look back at past performance and forward to future progress.

## ■ Knowing where we're coming from

For many schools, development planning starts with a review of school aims. Most schools have a list of aims which appears at the front of their prospectuses. In the effective school, these aims are used to define the ethos and activities of the school and are the starting point for any internal review. Many lists of aims which were written by way of statutory and rhetorical obligation, have now been rewritten with a sharper, defining purpose. Most important of all, in these schools, has been the rewording of aims in a way which can be subscribed to by all users – teachers, students, governors and parents. At best, these aims are precise, brief and written in a jargon-free language.

In some schools, a tortuous values debate has adversely affected staff morale. If too much time is taken in the process of consultation and exacting definition, the management team will not be seen to take decisive action. Assertive leadership can help forge a consensus agreement. Once agreed upon, these aims can be used as the starting point for annual, internal review. At Abbeydown School (the case study school in Section C), the headteacher audited the school in respect of its single unifying aim by deriving the indicators, or success criteria, which might reveal whether the school was achieving its aim:

- in classrooms;
- in corridors;
- in the curriculum;
- in the relationships between teachers and students;
- in the extra-curricular life of the school;
- in its means of communication.

In the first instance, teachers were asked to evaluate the school in respect of the indicators on a four-point scale where

1 = never apparent

2 = occasionally apparent

3 = frequently apparent

4 = always apparent

This was matched to a similar survey of attitudes among post-16 students. As a result, current performance was appraised and targets for improvement and priorities for development were acknowledged. Subsequently, the unifying aim and the leading objectives were used at Abbeydown as the starting point for whole-school and departmental review and development planning.

## ◼ Departmental review

Departmental review has been established in as many different ways as there are schools. In some instances, the headteacher informally interviews each head of department at the beginning of the academic year. In others, a pro-forma is provided (see Section D7) requiring comment on key areas of performance. Elsewhere, a line manager is responsible for leading a particular department through a review procedure. Whatever procedure has been adopted, to date, departmental review has placed little emphasis upon **evaluation of performance**.

The most effective school management teams support departments in their internal review and help them pose difficult questions about performance. A line management system which supportively allocates a particular member of the senior management team to a particular department ensures that more than lip-service is paid to departmental development planning.

Within the cycle of review, any department should be helped to evaluate its performance and assemble a review document in the first half of the first term of the academic year. Helped by the line manager, the review should locate between four and six areas for evaluation.

For example, a department might review its performance in respect of

- examination results

- assessment procedures

- schemes of work

- the use of information technology

- approaches to group work

Over the eight-week period, evidence is obtained from evaluation (see Section C2) to inform judgements.

The departmental head and line manager then write a development plan for the department which can:

- summarise performance in respect of the agreed areas for evaluation;

- highlight successes;

- draw attention to perceived areas for improvement;

- determine priorities in the short, medium and long term;

- indicate the resource implications.

A departmental review meeting then takes place at which the departmental development plan is discussed by departmental members in the presence of the line manager.

Ideally, individual departments submit their development plans to the senior management team at the end of October or beginning of November. The senior management team will gather their own evidence of whole-school performance through a review of its aims. On this basis, like individual departments, they will set priorities for future action.

The cumulative evidence from this half term of school evaluation can be gathered together as the school's development plan for the annual review meeting (see Section B6).

In line with one of the central principles of the 'good' school, such a development plan will be the result of collegial and collaborative work. As a result of all parties having been involved in the process of review,the school's priorities can be seen to be collective and acceptable.

## ◼ What the development plan looks like

A school development plan should be concise, accessible, easily understood by all users and, above all, useful. A document which is not opened from one annual review meeting to the next is of little use. A document which indicates directions for development and which is a reference point for action and evaluation throughout the year is clearly a working manual for school improvement.

The school development plan should have a statement of the school aims as its first page. In this way, the development plan starts from a collective vision of what the school stands for. It can then proceed, through evaluative evidence, to a statement of resource needs. A plan which proceeds from resources to implementation without these precursors pays little heed to development and improvement.

It is possible for the management team to link the development plan to the school's budget once priorities and resource needs have been identified. Thus, a growth budget should enable most priorities to be addressed; a reduced budget requires the governors' finance sub-committee to allocate expenditure on the basis of development plan priorities. Without a development plan, in a time of budget cuts, decisions may be made through expedience. There are schools whose managers say, in times of educational cuts, that their development plans are 'on the back burner'. Such a view is short-sighted. A commitment to review and development should be possible regardless of cuts; it is certainly desirable for staff morale that the school is seen to be managed in a forward-looking way. In any event, many developments have a modest resource implication.

Having decided on the annual priorities for action in the context of the school's budget, a summary statement may be appended to the development plan which states action for the school as a whole and departments in particular using the following pro-forma:

STATEMENT OF AIM:

TO BE MANAGED BY:

INVOLVING (personnel):

IMPLEMENTATION PLAN (including timescale):

RESOURCE NEEDS:

i) Development costs
ii) Running costs

SUCCESS CRITERIA (and any other evaluation data)

---

In times of change a development plan ensures coherence and reassures those who are being managed within a school that there is a direction and purpose. At the very least, the stated objectives for a given year make it clear what is to be expected and that no additional burdens will be imposed over the stated priorities for development.

# B3
# Using the school development plan

Some development plans we have seen have all the hallmarks of dust-collectors of the future. They were clearly written by the head or the senior management team over a weekend, and in response to external pressure – someone spotted that the Education Reform Act required schools to have a plan, or the LEA asked for a copy, or an inspection loomed.

A good school development plan is a live document, one which is an important and frequent source of reference for staff and other school constituents (B8), and a genuine support to them in their daily work. This section gives some ideas on how to make the development plan such a document.

The school development plan can be made live by:

- balancing vision with realism – pursuing lofty aims while taking a realistic approach to resources, including staff energy as well as money;

- using a format which promotes access – a contents table, clear lay-out, plain language, and a common one page format for each sub-plan (B3). The use of a single sheet summary such as that shown in figure 3 is invaluable. This summary will be issued to: all staff with their school planner/diary; governors and PTA, with their key school papers; partner schools and the LEA; as well as being displayed on notice boards;

- affixing a large copy to the staffroom wall, adding dates when targets were achieved and up-dating performance indicators showing how progress is being made in, for example, attendance. This can be a great motivator and ratify the value of the plan;

- referring to it at all meetings of staff and governors, particularly as a guide to decision-making. When faced with choices of action, refer overtly to the plan for guidance as to which action accords best with the priorities set. Themes for evaluation will be to a large extent determined by the plan;

- ensuring that people need to refer to it frequently, by incorporating into it the school aims, the budget, the action plan written following inspection (B9), and the targets from the annual review (B6). **All of these documents are the development plan. Schools which separate them miss the main point of the plan**, which is to ensure that there is a link between the values and aims of the school, its performance against them, its priorities for action to get nearer to fulfilling them, and the way resources will be used to enact those priorities. The plan is therefore a means of ensuring that the daily actions of the school contribute to realising its long-term aspirations;

- balancing whole-school and departmental plans within it. The planning process explained in B2 will mean that the geography department will need to respond to whole-school priorities such as assessment or study skills, as well as pursuing its own priorities such as a review of the department's fieldwork programme or map resources. The more it affects daily practice in the teaching subject, and the more it is the one place teachers have to look for guidance and information, the more chance the plan has to work. The skill for managers lies in keeping teachers' eyes also on whole-school targets, which they may not own quite so readily;

- managing the plan to a timescale which accords with the natural rhythm of the school year. Evaluation of year-end figures for exam results, student destinations and the budget, the 'freeze-frame' of the annual review, setting of the budget – all fit into the plan at their own time of year, and give opportunity for constant revisiting and fine-tuning the plan (D8);

- the use of the plan to *reject* a possible development. If we really believe in the planning process and in the priorities it has produced, we will reject or postpone a proposed development which

| PRIORITY AREA | DESCRIPTION OF DEVELOPMENT | MANAGED BY | INVOLVING | MILESTONES | BUDGET | NOTES |
|---|---|---|---|---|---|---|
| **Modern languages in key stage 4** | Development of modern language for all in Y10/11; new 5% course for less able | HoD ML | Dep Hd Curric; dept; HoD Eng & Hums | outline proposal to SMT by Dec; fully costed plan to Feb academic board. Implement Sept. | £200 for planning in current year £1200 start-up next f.y. permanent 5%+ to base budget | follows on from KS3 last year |
| **Curriculum continuity from Y6 to Y7** | Improve curriculum continuity with primary schools beginning with core NC subjects | Primary Hd will chair working party | Hds & Y6 tchrs in 6 key primaries; HoDs NC subjects  All staff | report to joint govs meeting Feb with draft action plan | £250 for working party to meet; each primary will add £50 | working party to include hd Y7, Y7 tutor, 3 HoDs, 2 primary heads, 2 Y6 teachers  MAJOR ITEM OF WHOLE-SCHOOL DEVT ARISING FROM EVALUATION |
| **Homework** | to investigate parental concerns and take any necessary action | Hd Y8 will chair group | all staff | findings to full staff and PTA mtg Feb; action plan by Mar. Some action immediate, some next academic year | £250 for group to meet | concern arising from parent questionnaire  group to include 4 teachers, 2 parents 1 primary teacher; will coopt students or involve year councils |

Figure 3   School development plan summary sheet

does not fit the plan, and which therefore threatens the health of the organisation by over-stretching its resources or by 'taking its eye off the ball';

- compiling the plan in such a way that the commitment of the constituents, especially the staff, to it is enhanced;

- providing evidence to school constituents of the quality of its planning, which promotes strength and coherence.

The way the plan is used depends on the reasons for its production in the first place. The frequency and quality of its use probably depends on the involvement of staff in its production. There are perhaps five reasons for writing the plan:

- to establish a **link** between the school's long-term aims and values, its short- to medium-term priorities, and the budget;

- to **focus** the limited time and energy of the school on a few priorities, rather than dissipating it on a large number;

- to provide a **rationale** for those priorities and consequent resource decisions. The increased accountability of heads and governors means that they often have to justify their decisions to a wide audience. A well-reasoned plan is a great support;

- to involve and **inform** the school's constituents – students, staff (teaching and non-teaching), governors, parents, community – and to gain their **commitment** to the priorities;

- to form a key component in the cycle of review and development (**quality** assurance – see A2).

Financial stringency has caused a number of schools to question the value of development planning. This comes about for two reasons:

1    The use of the word 'development' in the title of the plan, carries with it overtones of growth and improvement. When hard financial times arrive, some react against the plan, arguing that all their cherished plans for improvement will be thwarted by the lack of resources.

   Some schools respond by changing the title of their plan to 'management plan', 'business plan', or just 'plan'. It is as well to examine the overtone of each title before deciding which to use.

2    Development planning began in many areas with TVEI Extension, in a climate of growth. The purpose of the first plans was to show how TVEI objectives would be realised through the

extra cash the initiative brought. It has proved difficult for some to look afresh at the plan as a way of managing development in a time of no growth, or of cutback.

We believe that the antithesis is the case – that in a 'cold climate', the need for a good plan and a good planning process is heightened, for the following reasons:

1   What we now think of as a development plan takes on board the implications of LMS for greater resource-consciousness and greater school (head and governor) autonomy and accountability. Consequently, there is a greater emphasis on making, justifying and communicating management decisions.

2   The importance of planning is heightened in hard times because of the need to focus even more clearly on priorities, and to avoid a vacuum of unplanned activity in which unwise resource allocation is likely.

3   It is often said that both the product (the plan) and the process of assembling it have value, but that the latter is the more valuable. If this is so, then it is equally valuable in hard times as in good.

Some early development plans tended towards the high-minded rather than the practical – the 'values' rather than the 'budget priorities' end of the spectrum. Recently-produced plans begin to show a distinct shift the other way, and focus on the need to plan for maintaining the core functions of the school, as well as for enhancement. A good plan has both vision and practicality. If cuts go some way towards bringing vision and budget together in a realistic plan for the management of the school towards its goals within severe constraints, then some good will have resulted from the pain.

# B4
# Policy-making

 ## Introduction

Most schools have written policy statements to inform certain aspects of school life. It is common for schools to have, for example, a 'Behaviour policy', or, a 'Homework policy', or a 'Marking policy'. The purpose of these statements is to prescribe an outline for consistent and coherent activity by teachers and students. However, it is equally common for policy statements to be part of the institutional furniture and to be remote from the day-to-day life of the school. Consequently, schools often embark upon a 'policy review' which aims to breathe life into moribund policies and create fresh and purposeful statements that will inform the life of the school. The current external pressures on schools have led many management teams to recognise the need for more precise school policies designed to ensure coherence and, thus, maintain a sense of purpose and direction within the school and lead to heightened morale among teachers.

Of critical importance is the need to convert policy statements into good practice; practice, moreover, which is sustained over an extended period. In the experience of the authors, many management teams say: *'We feel we need a policy on 'X' but we're not quite sure how to arrive at it or what to do with it to make sure that it sticks!'* The following section aims to respond to this plea.

## ■ Deriving policy

The most important feature of any successful policy is the fact that it arises from a recognised, collective need; thus the teachers who are to put the policy into practice can subscribe to it. For example, concern among the staff of a school that students are not taking sufficient care over the production and handing-in of homework often leads to a collective sense that 'something needs to be done about this'. It is more difficult to create consensus policy when it is the management team of the school which senses that marking and assessment procedures are inconsistent. When presented with this view, teachers are likely to become defensive and unwilling to see that there is any need for fresh policy unless they are helped to recognise the need through the evidence of hard data. The gathering of hard data to aid self-evaluation is modelled at various stages in this book as the desirable prelude to successful management of change.

The example of a policy for marking and assessment may be taken further:

The cycle of internal review has suggested to the school's management team that there is a degree of inconsistency across the curriculum in respect of marking and assessment.

The team recognise the need to substantiate this through hard data, and, so, appoint a review body to look into practice within the school.

A representative group from across the curriculum is assembled, with a brief 'to review current approaches to marking and amendment in Key Stage 3'.

This group samples students' work, interviews and/or conducts a questionnaire survey of teachers and students to gain a picture of current practice. It is acknowledged that their review needs to be conducted with care over a long enough period to provide substance, but in sufficiently short order to have purpose.

When the evidence has been gathered, an objective report is presented to the staff as a whole. It is advisable to present a summary statement in advance of verbal feedback, giving staff an opportunity to question and comment. Assuming that the objective review confirms that there is a lack of consistency in marking and assessment, the management team is then able to move colleagues towards making consistent policy. As stated above, the overriding principle governing any policy is the fact that it can be realised in practice.

The first stage in converting an identified need into written policy is the statement of a clear **rationale** to underlie the policy. So, the review group might state the need for:

*An Assessment and Marking Policy which ensures that students' work is regularly assessed in a consistent way in all curriculum areas. The purpose behind all assessment is to aid student improvement. Thus, assessment should be formative and lead to the setting of individual targets which can be readily monitored.*

Given agreement to this basic rationale, the policy review group might be charged to produce a draft policy statement.

## Drafting a policy statement

1    Successful policy statements are concise, use unambiguous language and can be readily linked to identifiable practice. A policy statement which is longer than two or three sides of A4 is unlikely to be used as a working document.

2    Policy details should be grouped in a logical way and written under numbered cumulative points.

3    A policy statement should be accessible to all users, which includes parents and governors as well as teachers; therefore, the language should be exact and jargon-free.

4    Each point should be capable of answering the following question: 'How can we put this into practice?'

5   Once written, the draft policy statement should be presented to the staff as a whole in the same way as the evidence from the review would have been presented.

In some cases, it is advisable for two or three alternative policies to be drafted since this can often aid discussion and ensure that the adopted policy is the result of active consultation.

A consensus policy statement should be arrived at after reasonable consultation and debate. The more that the policy statement is seen to be the product of a representative review and drafting group, the more it is likely to be approved and accepted. The least effective policy statements are those which are drafted and imposed by senior management teams.

## ■ Implementing policy

A statement of policy which is the result of whole-staff agreement, is of little value unless it is wedded to a phased implementation plan. As a consequence, the senior management team, in consultation with the review group, should draw up short-, medium- and long-term plans together with key stages for evaluation.

Within a fortnight of the acceptance of the policy, a plan should be published which states what should be enacted: by the end of term; by the end of the year; during next year. To take the working example, it may be decided that all teachers will mark according to a prescribed code by the *end of term*; that each department will have reviewed and implemented a profiling system for Year 7 *by the end of the year*; and that all students will have regular target-setting meetings with their tutors *by next year*. In addition to the implementation plan, there must be prescribed points and approaches to evaluation in order for the senior management team to assure itself that progress is being made and that the policy is improving practice.

Evaluation can be undertaken at significant points by the policy review team who can use the same approaches as those used for their initial survey as a way of assessing progress and improvement. Little true evaluation can take place without the evidence of an initial survey since it then becomes impossible to measure the added value of a new policy or approach.

Making an excessive number of policy statements at any one point is ill-advised. In some instances, schools have undertaken a policy review and written or rewritten a large number of policies at one fell swoop. Under these circumstances, the resulting paperwork does little to inform practice. Policy statements that descend in a blizzard and are not wedded to a cycle of review; consultation; implementation planning and continuous evaluation tend to be consigned to wastepaper bins and filing cabinets. Policy should be reviewed as a consequence of a recognisable need; as a result, no more than four policies should be reviewed in any one school year.

## B5
# What performance indicators are useful?

Classroom management and students' learning are subtle and sophisticated matters, not to be reduced to a set of crude numerical measures. However, every individual and organisation needs to know how it is doing, and schools cannot hide away from scrutiny of their achievements. In order to anchor their development plans firmly, schools need feedback on performance. Heads and governors therefore need good quality management information which enhances the school's self-evaluation, planning and development, and which may be used, alongside the other components of quality assurance in the model in A2, to monitor and report the school's achievements.

The term **performance indicator** has been used indiscriminately to include

- numerical data, both those which are descriptive (such as numbers on roll) and those which involve value judgement (such as the presentation of examination statistics);

- qualitative aspects, such as the leadership qualities of the head-teacher;

- measures of input, process and outcome.

We propose that schools need two types of performance indicator:

1  **School profile data** – a set of quantitative measures in those areas which are of such importance that they must be tracked to provide comparison year on year and, if available through the collection of such data to standard specification, across schools with which comparison would be appropriate and helpful. These

standard quantitative data are analogous to a record of achievement or summative profile for the school – hence the use of the term **school profile** for the assembled array of data.

2   **Institution-derived indicators** – the criteria which will be used to evaluate the effectiveness of key objectives in the development plan, built into that plan ab initio as **success criteria**. These indicators are analogous to targets in formative profiling. Each objective should have at least one indicator; many, if not all, will be quantitative. Schools can no more manage a vast number of such indicators than the number of development priorities that they would represent. (Success criteria are dealt with in more detail in B7.)

It is worth putting in some **health warnings** at this point:

1   'Statistical performance indicators can monitor certain facets of a school's performance . . . but these are no substitute for a well-organised system of professional quality assurance.' (Audit Commission, **Managing Services Effectively – Performance Review**, 1989, para 49)

2   Since most data need interpretation, they are liable to misinterpretation. Most data only come to have meaning when compared through time or space. Although we must not assume those reading the data are simple-minded, lacking in common-sense or malicious, caution over publication and access is needed.

3   Indicators do just that – they indicate, opening a debate, not closing it with a judgement. They indicate aberrance and open an enquiry into it.

4   The choice of data is value-laden. The collection of data affects behaviour as well as measuring it – it will be vital to ensure that the effects are benign.

5   'Gresham's Law' – that the measurable drives out the non-measurable, and that the aim of performance review is diverted away from increasing effectiveness towards reducing or enlarging the costs – must be avoided; numerical data should be put into their rightful place as but one part of the assessment of the health of the organisation.

Since 'success criteria' as defined above are by definition idiosyncratic, this section proposes only a suite of 'school profile data' (Figure 4). No great skill with using or interpreting statistics is implied – there may be heads and governors who wish to use multi-level modelling to look at their results, but what is given here is a basic set of suggestions.

| WEEKLY/MONTHLY INDICATORS | | PARTY RESPONSIBLE |
|---|---|---|
| Attendance rate (pupils) | • %, by year, to national specification | tutors, totalled by office staff |
| Attendance rate (staff) | • %, breakdown by illness/staff development | member of staff ic cover |
| Budget | • % of budget spent, against anticipated profile | bursar |

**ANNUAL INDICATORS**

| | | |
|---|---|---|
| Student data | • number on roll, by year, as % of school standard number | school office |
| | • eligible for free school meals % | |
| | • those for whom English is their 2nd language | |
| | • applications: admissions | heads year 7/12 |
| Test/Exam data | • (including KS2 & 3 SATs) see B3 for schedule | ic exams |
| | • SATs results: % in each level | year head/primary partners |
| | • Reading age of intake (implies common test) | primary partners |
| | • value-added (added competence): average SATs level increment KS 2 to 3, 3 to 4; average increment for each initial level, to ascertain achievement across ability range | year/KS heads |
| Destination data | • from Y11 to Y12, % to 6th, FE, employment, YT, other | ic Careers, year heads, County Careers Service |
| | • from Y13 (ditto minus YT, plus HE) | |
| Curriculum data | • hours/week taught | timetabler |
| | • % of curriculum time to each NC subject, by year | timetabler |
| Staff data | • % on allowances A-E, by gender | school office |
| | • ratio of teaching: non-teaching | school office |
| | • contact ratio | timetabler |
| | • PTR/average class size, by year | timetabler |
| Budget data | • % spent on: teaching staff, non-teaching staff, premises-related, students, other | bursar |
| | • planned against outturn in these categories | bursar |
| | • unit cost | bursar |
| Parental data | • amount contributed cf other sources | bursar |
| | • % attending parents' evenings, by year | year heads |
| Premises data | • energy costs/pupil | bursar/caretaker |
| | • redecoration cycle | bursar/caretaker |
| | • value of self-help schemes | bursar |

Figure 4    Performance indicators

Wherever possible, these data should be compared through time within the school, with local schools with whom comparison is useful, and with LEA and national figures. The list has been chosen so as to represent the key areas under which a school could be said to 'perform'; it has been kept as short as reasonably possible so as not to clutter either the head's desk or the senior management team/Governors' review and planning. Clearly, the performance of individual departments and units within the school will be of interest; these are considered in C2 and C12.

In deciding which of these the school will collect, the head will need to consider:

- What will I use the data for?

- To whom and how do I therefore need to publish them?

The head of one school found that the attendance rate of Y10 students was significantly below what he expected and the other schools in the area achieved. His sole (and successful) strategy for increasing attendance was to raise the profile of attendance. He published the school's figures weekly on the staffroom notice board, insisted that tutors follow up unsupported absence, and raised the issue of attendance at staff meetings, stressing the obvious point that none of the worthy curricular aims of the school could be achieved for absent students.

# B6
# Holding an annual review meeting

## ▣ Introduction

The development planning cycle is concerned with a continuous process of evaluation, review, prioritising, action planning and implementation. Within this continuous process it is desirable to take stock and review the progress of the school at a critical point. The annual review meeting provides such an opportunity for reflection and target-setting.

The logical point in the year when the review meeting should take place would seem to be towards the end of the first term of the academic year. At this point performance data will have been assembled and analysed, specific evaluations can have taken place and the development plan should have been reviewed.

## ■ Assembling the data for the meeting

A review meeting is concerned with two simple purposes: opportunities to look back at previous performance and to look forward to future action. Consequently, the most important piece of evidence will be the targets from the previous review meeting (if such a meeting has taken place). In any event, the school must ask itself two very simple questions concerning the previous year:

- What did we set out to achieve?

- To what extent have we been successful in meeting these aims?

By the end of the first half of the first term of the academic year, most schools can gather reliable data concerning performance and management during the previous year. Thus, it is possible to assemble the following statistical data prior to the annual review:

- Student entry attainments

- Examination performance

- Post-16 and post-18 destinations

- Attendance rates

- Budgetary out-turn figures

- Staffing structure

- Staff deployment

- Age and sex profile of staff

In some, if not all, cases it is possible to gather comparative data from other or similar schools within a Local Education Authority. It is then possible for aspects of performance to be scrutinised in the context of performance elsewhere. As has been stated, the use of any such data will merely offer an opportunity to investigate performance on the basis of these indicators; it does not provide the absolute truth about a school's performance.

Obviously, the main business of a school is the management of the curriculum. Any review meeting must look at the curriculum in organisational terms as well as in terms of examination performance. Consequently, the relevant forms which summarise the disposition of time and organisation of groups for the teaching of the National Curriculum at Key Stage 3 and Key Stage 4 are necessary review meeting documents. The summary papers from the individual department development plans will be required, since they provide data concerning performance as well as the findings from targeted evaluation. As a working document, the school development plan should be available for the review meeting. As mentioned in Section B2, this should contain the results of whole school evaluations in respect of aims and a statement of perceived priorities for the coming year.

The paperwork having been assembled, the school is in a position to derive a precise fourfold agenda which itemises areas for particular scrutiny:

1   Review of previous targets

2   Performance data

3   Curriculum review

4   Development plan priorities

## ■ The participants and conduct of the meeting

The annual review meeting should be taken as an opportunity to focus the work of those internal and external parties who participate in the management of the school. It is, clearly, important for the senior management team of the school to be present in its entirety since those individuals are responsible for the line management of the school. In addition, representatives of the governing body should be present; at best, the chairs of the finance sub-committee and the curriculum sub-committee. Where appropriate, the LEA officer attached to the school and the school's inspector may be on hand to offer comparative data and detailed advice concerning evaluations which they have undertaken in the school during the previous year.

The chairing of the meeting from amongst this group should be decided well in advance. The chair should rest with the person who is most able to exercise the objective functions of a chairperson. Those who need to give evidence or engage in developmental debate should not be required to chair the meeting. Consequently, the headteacher and the line managers should not chair the meeting. The chairperson should be someone who has a wide understanding of all aspects of education and is able to lead discussions and involve all parties.

The annual review meeting is the focus point of the year and should be given an appropriate slice of uninterrupted time. A reasonable length of time to enable each of the agenda items to be given due attention would seem to be three hours or half a day. Keeping official minutes from which targets can be derived is essential. It may be that this function can fall to the school's Education Officer from the LEA, or a chosen external consultant.

## ■ The consequence of the annual review meeting

The main purpose of the meeting will have been to take stock, look forwards and set targets. Targets will need to be agreed as a supplement to the perceived priorities of the development plan. These targets will reach in a variety of directions and be appropriate to all of those present at the meeting. It is a mistake to set targets for any one who was not present at the meeting. A record of the targets with the initials of the person to whom each target applies is necessary. Thus, action can be taken by the headteacher, the line managers, representatives of the governing body, representative of the LEA, or the school's consultant.

Since this meeting will have involved key people for a lengthy part of the school day, it is essential that all teaching and non-teaching staff are presented with a verbal summary of the meeting together with the written statement of targets. This feedback should take place as soon after the meeting as possible.

The focus provided by the annual review meeting may influence priorities on the school development plan. Given a review meeting towards the end of the first term, the development plan should be able to be amended and agreed well in advance of the budget matching exercise of the governing body.

# B7
# Target-setting, success criteria and implementation plans

## ■ Target-setting

The most immediate product arising from the review of the school's development plan is a series of targets for future action. A target is a quantifiable measure which, it is hoped, will improve performance. **Target-setting** is the process of determining the specific goals that are to be achieved over a defined period.

Targets may be set by the senior management team for the school as a whole; by a department for its work; or by an individual teacher in respect of performance in the classroom. It is usual for targets to be set at the end of the cycle of review; this might be at the department or school's annual review meeting or the teacher's appraisal interview. Targets can very often be two-way: the school sets itself a target to help a teacher who sets him/herself a target for improved performance.

Some targets are related to budgetary provision, such as,

- the allocation of additional funding for resources in history and geography;
- the provision of audio-visual hardware for modern languages.

Others are linked to improvements in performance, such as,

- a decrease in absences by Y9 students;
- an increase in student retention on educational courses post-16.

Less quantifiable are the targets which are allied to the statement of policy, such as:

- the establishment of an assessment policy.

More elusive are those targets which are concerned with aspects of teaching and learning, like,

- a coordinated approach to the development of reading in Y7.

## ■ Success Criteria

Even the most apparently straightforward of targets, such as the modern languages department's commitment to ensuring that all Key Stage 3 students have a visit to France, needs to be related to success criteria. It is not enough to state, in this example, that the success criteria will be that all children go to France since this in itself does not assure a quality experience. Underlying the department's commitment to this venture may be their desire to ensure that all students

- purchase goods at a shop;
- ask for directions in a town;
- order refreshments in a cafe.

These might constitute the barest success criteria for the trip, which would need to be monitored and evaluated to assure the quality of the experience.

Success criteria, then, are those indicators which help the management of a school recognise that real progress has been made in respect of agreed targets. There is little point in agreeing targets within the school without establishing the bench-marks which will monitor their achievement. With appropriate success criteria, it is possible to set intermediate targets and determine an implementation plan which will ensure commitment and maintain motivation. Staff morale is adversely affected when targets are set and implemented halfheartedly between annual review meetings. It is important to allocate a particular manager for the implementation of particular targets so that a named person is seen to be responsible for the monitoring and evaluation of each of them.

## ■ Success criteria and implementation plans

The following success criteria might be established in respect of some of the targets set above. Very often, the success criteria will amount to the outline of an implementation plan.

Thus, in the following examples, success is likely to be identified when the listed points have been implemented.

---

### A decrease in absences by Y9 students

1 The scrutiny of weekly absence patterns for the last year

2 The monitoring by tutors of parental absence notes

3 The maintenance of spot checks by the educational welfare officer

4 The implementation of lesson registration

5 The establishment of an acceptable rewards system for good attendance by a tutor group

6 The publication of monthly attendance rates for tutor groups.

Managed by: *The head of lower school*

---

### An increase in student retention on educational courses post-16

1 An examination of retention and success rates on particular courses over the previous five years

2 A survey of current post-16 student attitudes towards their courses

3 A review and modification of current post-16 course provision

4    A survey of current Year 11 students' expectations for their post-16 and post-18 futures

5    An improved guidance procedure for post-16 courses

6    The establishment of a relevant and appropriate induction programme to improve progression on to post-16 courses

7    The evolution of an approach to individual student action planning.

Managed by: *The head of upper school*

---

### A coordinated approach to the development of reading in Y7

1    The establishment of a 'Language and learning' working party

2    A survey of the current experience of reading for Y7 students

3    The determination of the reading needs that are required by curriculum areas

4    The provision of staff development time to encourage the involvement and responsibility of all teachers in the development of reading

5    The provision of support and guidance from the special needs department

6    The allocation of specific approaches to reading to particular curriculum areas and teachers

7    A communication to parents of the school's commitment to the development of reading and the role that parents might play

8    The regular monitoring of the students' weekly experience of reading and the communication of this data to staff.

Managed by: *The Language and Learning Working Party*

---

# ■ Achievable targets and management credibility

Considerable care and time needs to be invested to ensure that agreed targets are monitored and achieved. It is essential, therefore, that a manageable number of targets is set for whole school and departmental development. Anything in excess of six targets for the school or for each department will become unwieldy. Most serious of all, is the fact that excessive targets are unlikely to be realised in a substantial and developmental way. The victim under these circumstances is managerial credibility. If a school does not bother to establish success criteria with which to frame the implementation plan for its agreed targets, these will make minimal impact in its commitment to school improvement.

# B8
# Obtaining feedback from constituents

Figure 2 in section A2 shows 'feedback from constituents' (governors, parents, the community, students) as a key part of the quality assurance process. Obtaining the opinions of those who have an interest in the school has two purposes:

- to diminish the possibility of complacency or myopia. The institution must not be blind to the opinions of informed 'outsiders', many of whom are its customers;

- to be seen as a responsive, open organisation, one which seeks the views of its constituents and takes note of them.

That is not to say that the school acts on *every* view expressed – part of the value of systematic and open dialogue is that it reveals the paradoxical views of different parts of the constituency, and makes it clear that the school needs the wisdom of Solomon to resolve these conflicts to everyone's satisfaction.

The process of consultation begins with the definition of the constituent groups. The term 'constituent' is used to give as broad a scope as possible. The business community would refer to its 'clients', 'customers' or 'consumers'; these terms pose real difficulties to schools, for two reasons:

1    Education has no simple producer–consumer relationship. Is the product the school, and the consumer the parent who may choose among schools?
    *or*
    Is the product the student, and the consumer 'society', in which s/he plays the roles of partner, parent, employee etc?

*or*

Is the product the curriculum, and the consumer the student?

The answer to each of these is 'yes', but, since schools get their resources largely by attracting students, it is likely that they will have to treat parents as their chief customers.

2   Whereas in business the customer is king, this is not the case in education. A more valid analogy might be the health service, where the technical expertise of a doctor comes together with the personal experience and vested interest of the patient to effect a healthy future.

Some constituent groups are listed below, but it is strongly recommended that the school think carefully and laterally to create its own list which will fulfil both objectives above.

[In addition to the school teaching staff, who are the 'insiders' in the process.]

Students
Non-teaching staff
Parents
Governors
Partner schools/colleges –
- parallel
- preceding
- succeeding

LEA –
- officers
- inspectors

SEN network
Youth service
Careers service
Training and Enterprise Council/education-business partnership/business community
Health/welfare/social services groups
Community – the town

Having defined the objectives and the participant groups – the 'why' and the 'who' – it is necessary to fix the 'what, how and when'.

- On what do we require feedback (and on what do people want to give us feedback)?

- When do we want it?

- How do we go about getting it?

- Is it realistic to get feedback from every group on everything? If not, how do we select?

The answer to the question 'On what should we consult our constituents?' lies partly in the stage of the school's development, and partly in its development plan.

## Stage of development

Obtaining the views of constituents improves with practice – the school gets better at asking, and the constituents better at answering in ways which are useful. This argues for a systematic process over time, in which the constituents become used to being asked, and indeed expect it and are indignant when it does not happen. Early in the process, some schools have used one of two approaches:

- a whole-school review, perhaps part of the assembly of the first development plan (B2), which helps the school focus on a small number of areas for development which all groups agree on. The question 'What makes a good school?' (B1) is posed to teachers, parents, students and governors. An agreed schedule is drawn up from all responses, and then comments invited on how the school measures up to each item in the schedule;

- the review of an aspect of the school on which a wide constituency will have strong and useful views: homework is a good example. Others such as dress are possible, but politically fraught!

## School development plan

As the consultation process becomes more established, the priorities in the Development Plan give the agenda for evaluation of performance, and it becomes second nature to involve the wider audience in this process. Selecting the appropriate group(s) to consult on any given issue also becomes more straightforward – but don't always use the obvious links. For example, non-teaching staff may have interesting and insightful views on work experience, not just the more obvious business partners. It is worth remembering that some constituents will want to give views on matters other than those on which you wish to consult, and that their voice should be heard.

Opinions may be obtained in three main ways. Questionnaires and interviews are considered in D2. Meetings may also be valuable. Choosing a technique involves deciding on the size of sample and the level of detail required. Is a brief questionnaire survey of a large population best, or a detailed set of interviews of a few people? Or would a broad discussion at a meeting followed by detailed interviews of a few key people be best? What time can we afford?

Two points are worth remembering:

1   You are not trying to produce results which are statistically valid. Although this is not an excuse for sloppy thinking and clearly biased results, educationists do tend to intellectualise and argue about validity rather than just listening to a good spread of views.

2   Persist; although it is well known that 10% of letters from schools to parents actually get home, and that most of them have been through the washing machine before they are read, consultation does become more successful the more those consulted are used to it. There are creative ways of reaching a bigger audience:

   • publicising the request for information in the newsletter;

   • linking the request for information with an invitation;

   • asking parents at parents' evenings to complete your question-naire (this will be selective, but attendance at intake, Y7 and Y9 parents' evenings is very high);

   • dividing up the parent population into random groups and consulting each in rotation by letter posted to home.

Consulting students is easier in a structure of year/house/school councils. It is also more convincing to talk of strong links between the school and the community if there is a clear effort to create and nurture the community *within* the school through such means of student participation.

# B9
# Managing external inspection

Under new legislation, schools will be liable to much more regular and systematic inspection than has previously been the case in many areas of the country. It may seem a contradiction in terms to speak of the school 'managing' an inspection which is external, and the format of which is nationally determined. It is therefore in large measure imposed and managed from without.

However, governors may play some role in choosing and briefing the inspection team, and the report is in the first instance to those governors. In a well-managed school, the report will bring a lot of insights and confirming evidence, but no great surprises. The report therefore feeds data into your review and development programme. There is a requirement upon governors to produce and publish an action plan to show how the school will respond to the report's findings. This document is part of the school development plan (B2 and 3). We have said on more than one occasion that it is vital that the school works to one set of targets, and that inspection recommendations, the results of self-evaluation, feedback and performance data – all the components of the quality cycle in A2 – are brought together into the single development plan. Here they form the meat in the sandwich – a reasoned and prioritised set of targets reflecting the basic aims of the school on one side and reflected in the budget on the other.

If the school finds the inspection process an intrusion and a distraction, the odds are it will reject or marginalise the findings. School and inspectorate may get into an unproductive wrangle about the balance of the report and how 'typical' the period of the inspection was. **A competent inspectorate will share with the school the determination to secure improvement from the inspection as well as give the school a health check**.

The school can manage the inspection at three points:

1    By the choice of inspection team. Governors need a checklist against which to read tenders or protocols, and to interrogate their authors; such a checklist is given in Figure 5.

2    By preliminary negotiation with the reporting (registered, lead) inspector, to ensure that the inspection, as well as meeting the national framework, is geared to the needs of the school. A checklist for this process is given in Figure 6.

3    By writing the action plan in a way which, while it confronts the issues in the inspection report in an honest way, particularly those which are uncomfortable, embeds the response in the school development plan and gives the school ownership of the planned action. Some ideas are given below.


## ■ Writing the action plan: some helpful ideas

1    Governors have the responsibility of compiling an action plan to respond to the contents of the report. The inspectorate may not be involved directly in the compilation of this plan, but their oral

| Consideration | Comment on tenders |
|---|---|
| a The team used previously. Are the arguments for continuity – follow-up to last inspection and familiarity – outweighed by the desirability of a fresh view? | |
| b **Reputation** among local heads/governors of each team for a quality service, defined as:<br>– professional standards of conduct<br>– breadth of team and quality of membership<br>– quality of insight<br>– sensitivity<br>– delivery to specification, on time<br>– clarity of presentation, both oral and written<br><br>In the absence of such local reputation, is the background of team members what we would want as inspectors of our school? | |
| c **Skills** of teams in areas of particular interest to our school, namely . . .<br><br>**Attributes** of inspectors which may be of importance, eg their gender/ethnic mix to reflect that of the school | |
| d **The** tender itself:<br><br>presentation<br><br>number of inspector days proposed<br><br>number of inspectors and their mix of generalist/specialist skills<br><br>language – does it give the impression of a quick health check or of a commitment to secure improvement?<br><br>how does each tender deal with the issue of negotiation with the school? Is there a willingness to use the school development plan and school priorities as well as the national framework?<br><br>who will the lay inspector be, what is her/his background and skills, and what role will s/he play?<br><br>what assurances are given concerning the reporting procedure?<br><br>price: how does the overall deal compare with others? | |
| e **Follow-up**: does the tender suggest that support to the school is available in a way which does not compromise the integrity of the inspection? How do any such proposals stand up to the same scrutiny as a–d above? | |

Figure 5    Checklist for those considering tenders for school inspection

**Parents' meeting:**

[the lead inspector must meet with such members of the parent body as wish to do so, prior to the inspection]

To what extent does the registered inspector see this meeting as informing parents of the conduct and timescale of the inspection, and to what extent an opportunity to gain their views?

Will s/he take account of parents' views in shaping the fine detail of the inspection?

**School priorities:**

Will the registered inspector go through the School Development Plan with the head in order to familiarise her/himself with the school's priorities etc.?

What issues do we want the inspectorate to look at particularly closely?

What assurances can the registered inspector give that these matters will receive attention?

How can the school help with data, support?

How will the registered inspector convey these priorities to her/his team members?

Figure 6    School priorities: a checklist for heads/governors negotiating with the registered/lead/reporting inspector

report may be very helpful in formulating recommendations from their comments, and in obtaining their view of priorities within those recommendations. Make sure that you press the inspectorate for such advice at the oral report stage.

2    Recommendations are not requirements, unless the school is in breach of the law, in respect for example of the National Curriculum or of Health and Safety. The school should put the report of the inspection alongside the development plan priorities and the results of self-evaluation programmes.

- Where the two are agreed on the need to celebrate achievement and quality, a comment to that effect and a programme for further enhancement and dissemination should go into the action plan.

- Similarly, where the two are agreed on the need for remedial action, for example on the performance of the mathematics department, such action must form part of the action plan.

- Where the two take a contrary view of the same aspect, the action plan must contain the commitment to further, honest internal evaluation, and to appropriate follow-up action should the inspectorate be proved right.

| Area | Need for action | Proposed action | By whom/ by when | How/when evaluated |
|---|---|---|---|---|
| Mathematics | disseminate excellent practice with very able students | • seminar for HoDs | Head Maths next HoDs mtg | |
| | | • visits to lessons | each dept summer term | self-evaluation programme next yr. How well is the new policy helping identify and promote the needs of the most able? |
| | | • write school policy | Deputy head autumn term. (Hd of Maths to advise) | |
| Attendance in Y10/11 | increase to local average or beyond | • daily monitoring | tutors | LEA) figures |
| | | • letter to parents | head | EWO) |
| | | • follow-up absence | yr heads/EWO - immediate | monthly check |
| Geography | inspectors find dull, repetitive tasks in lessons and demotivated students. Our own internal evaluation disagrees with this, and so ... | | | |
| | further detailed investigation of classroom practice | • employ consultant<br>• department to log a sample of lessons etc | dep head to lead internal investigation in summer term | consultant's report<br><br>data from internal investigation exam results |

Figure 7   School action plan

The action plan is thereby incorporated into the School development plan, and the school takes ownership of the results of the inspection.

3   Parents, by receiving a summary of the report and a copy of the governors' action plan, and having them discussed with them at the governors' AGM, have the information to enable them to press the school for action to respond to areas of weakness. An honest approach to this is to produce an action plan which is clear and in plain English, and which commits the school to action. We propose an action plan such as that in Figure 7.

# Improving performance

## C1
## Improving the effectiveness of teaching and learning

### ■ Introduction

Although seduced into other managerial priorities, all headteachers acknowledge that the most important aspect of their schools is the quality of teaching and learning within their classrooms. Many headteachers also recognise that this is the aspect of their schools which they know least well because their time is spent in other areas of school management.

Throughout Section C, we take a case study example of 'one' representative school – Abbeydown School – whose headteacher seeks to respond to current managerial priorities. In her first year in a new appointment, she felt that her first priority was to assure herself of the quality of teaching and learning across curriculum areas. She shared this view with the staff and mounted a wide-ranging evaluation of classroom methodologies over a half-term period. From this evaluation she was able to help the staff of Abbeydown to derive a 'Teaching and learning policy' (B4) which was closely linked to the development needs of the school.

In order to ensure a high level of staff commitment the head was careful to brief all staff about her purpose and ensure that an appropriate and credible evaluation team was assembled. The time-scale for the enquiry, together with the date when reports would be made and outcomes achieved, was carefully negotiated and made clear to all who would be affected.

### ■ The evaluation team and the stages of the enquiry

The headteacher presented to the staff of Abbeydown School her view that there was an urgent need to examine teaching and learning styles. She felt that a consistent approach to this crucial element of school management should be underpinned by a clearly-stated and understood 'Teaching and learning policy'. She affirmed that she proposed to give time for rigorous evaluation of current practice. The evaluation team would comprise:

- a representative of each of the four faculties in Abbeydown;
- a probationary teacher;
- a member of the governing body;
- an external consultant (a member of the LEA advisory service);
- the headteacher.

After due consultation, it was agreed that the enquiry would consist of the following evaluative methods:

- student pursuits;
- interviews with a sample of staff;
- questionnaire of student perceptions;
- questionnaire of parental perceptions;
- matching to quality criteria.

The outcomes of the enquiry were staged as follows:

1   A summary of the findings from student pursuits:

2   A triangulation exercise among student, staff and parent perceptions;

3   An interim survey report;

4   A statement of the school's current practice when matched to quality criteria;

5   The writing of a concise 'Teaching and learning policy' to be understood by all users;

6   Continued faculty-based evaluation of the 'Teaching and learning policy';

7   A whole-school annual review of the effectiveness of classroom teaching and learning.

### ■ Student pursuits

All members of the evaluation team conducted a sample of classroom observations. Consequently, each team member conducted two student pursuits. Each member followed a student in Key Stage 3 and 4 for a full day. During each student pursuit, team members gathered hard data concerning the nature of the teaching and learning by using a pro-forma (see Section D1). The pursuits were completed over a three week period.

Each teacher whose lesson(s) was observed was guaranteed feedback by the observer. Feedback was consistently non-judgmental and amounted to discussion of the hard data from which the observed teacher was invited to draw further observations.

Once completed, the data from the 16 student pursuits was summarised and a statement was reported back to staff which showed the sample findings concerning the experience of students in each of the school's years. Data was available concerning:

- the distribution of time through a 'typical' day;
- the learning environment;
- the relationship between teachers and students;
- the nature of questioning across the curriculum;
- the experience of reading and writing across the curriculum;
- the experience of group-work and talk across the curriculum;
- the experience of girls and boys.

Faculties were required to examine the implications of this sample before reporting their observations back to a full staff meeting. Unresolved questions were reported to the evaluation team who produced a series of questionnaires and a structured interview pro-forma with which to further the enquiry.

## ■ Questionnaires and structured interviews

The questions that the staff of Abbeydown School wished to resolve as a result of the student pursuits were addressed on an individual teacher basis by mutual observation. This led, in turn, to some action research projects (see Section D6).

The evaluation team sought to further the enquiry through the use of simple questionnaires to students and their parents. A questionnaire was designed which gathered data concerning student attitudes and perceptions, for the most part, on a four-point scale. A further open-ended question was used to gauge specific observations. A parallel questionnaire was designed and administered at parents' evenings.

The attitudes and opinions gathered from the questionnaires were further supplemented by structured interviews with a sample of staff from all areas of the curriculum, chosen to represent a variety of experience within the school (see Section D2).

The evaluation team, having gathered the data, summarised their findings by triangulating the views of the three parties. A full staff meeting was given to the presentation of the interim survey report.

## ■ Matching to quality criteria

The external consultant in the evaluation team provided a set of quality criteria, written as four-point positional statements (see Section D3). The evaluation team took the data from their enquiry and sought to match Abbeydown School to the bank of statements in the quality criteria for 'Effective Teaching and Learning' (see below). The resulting 'Profile of teaching and learning at Abbeydown School' provided an acceptable statement of the school's current provision. Individual faculties were required to produce an action plan on the strength of the survey to date.

### A bank of quality criteria to evaluate the effectiveness of teaching and learning.

The following criteria headings and positional statements may be useful when evaluating the effectiveness of teaching and learning in the classroom:

#### 1 The timetable arrangements

**1.1** The length of lessons and their distribution through the week makes it difficult for teachers to range the learning experiences in a fashion which allows them to cater for individual needs.

**1.2** Although the length of lessons allows for variety in teaching and learning, their distribution through the week is haphazard and limits continuity of experience.

**1.3** Lessons are of appropriate length and well-distributed through the week.

**1.4** As well as being of appropriate length and well-distributed through the week, lessons are also timetabled in a way which encourages cooperation with other curriculum areas.

#### 2 The provision of resources for teaching

**2.1** There are no clearly developed schemes of work for the department; the teacher depends upon his/her own resources since departmental resources are stored and booked haphazardly.

**2.2** The teacher has access to teaching resources which support rudimentary schemes of work. In addition, the teacher has produced some resources for his/her own use and has stored them in her/his teaching base.

**2.3** The teacher can rely upon plentiful and accessible departmental resources which have been acquired and developed to complement the schemes of work for particular year groups. The library is used by the teacher from time to time.

**2.4** As well as the resources available at departmental level, the teacher is well-supported by a school resources centre which provides additional material through the knowledgeable school librarian.

## 3 The classroom environment

**3.1** The teacher has no single teaching base and, as a consequence, has to rely upon inconsistent classroom environments. For the most part, previous users leave the classroom tidy. Resources have to be brought to the classroom by the teacher.

**3.2** The classroom is tidy and well-organised. Some resources are available and limited commercial display is apparent. Furnishings are rigid and militate against a variety of learning styles.

**3.3** Resources are well-stored in the tidy and attractive learning environment. Good use is made of display material which includes some students' work. Flexible furnishings have been suitably arranged to allow for a variety of approaches to teaching and learning.

**3.4** The welcoming environment actively encourages a student-centred approach to learning. Resources are plentiful and accessible for students' autonomous use. Information technology is a frequent part of the students' experience within the classroom. Students' work is valued, displayed to advantage and regularly updated. Flexible furnishing ensures that the classroom can be used in a variety of ways to suit the learning objectives.

## 4 The provision of resources for students' use

**4.1** Most work undertaken by students takes place through the use of text-books or apparatus which leads to teacher-focused activity.

**4.2** Undifferentiated worksheets/workcards have been produced to supplement text-books and apparatus so that students can work on their own or with others.

**4.3** Students have been taught to make autonomous and responsible use of resources which are readily accessible to them within the classroom.

**4.4** Students can be relied upon to manage their own learning, at times, and have wide access to resources within and beyond the classroom. They are supported by sensitive curriculum tutoring which monitors and profiles this flexible approach to learning.

## 5 The relationship between teacher and students

**5.1** The teacher has tentative control over the students. Inattention is characteristic of the lesson, with several students speaking out of turn in a fashion which is disrespectful of peers and teacher alike. Consequently many students take little pride in their work. Sanctions are used inconsistently by the teacher.

**5.2** Students are well-behaved and follow instructions fully. There is little talk within the lesson apart from the teacher. Control is maintained through the exercise of well-understood sanctions. There is little contact between teacher and individual students.

**5.3** The relaxed and purposeful atmosphere is the consequence of mutual respect between teacher and students. The teacher controls the pace and rigour of the learning through a sensitive understanding of tone. The teacher knows the class as individuals and deals with students on an individual basis.

**5.4** Students have a clear sense of what the teacher expects from them; they are attentive to others, take pride in their work and behave in a responsible fashion when managing their own learning. The teacher makes much use of genuine praise, respects individual contributions and caters for the needs of each student. The atmosphere is one of trust and openness.

## 6 The planning and preparation of the lesson

**6.1** The lesson continues from work accomplished during the previous lesson. Materials are commercially produced and require standard responses across the ability range within the class.

**6.2** The lesson has clearly defined learning objectives which are shared with students at the lesson's start. Teaching materials have been acquired or prepared which seek to support and extend the learning.

**6.3** The lesson has been clearly planned as a series of cumulatively focused learning experiences which extend the basic objectives. A range of resources have been made available which provide varied stimuli for appropriate stages in the lesson.

**6.4** The careful planning of the lesson allows a flexibility which enables the teacher to manage the class as a whole and yet cater for individual needs. This is helped by the use of a range of resources which can be targeted at individual student needs.

## 7 The range of teaching and learning experiences

**7.1** The lesson focuses upon the teacher and involves much instruction and classroom discussion followed by the writing up of the taught experience.

**7.2** Following an initial teacher input, the lesson proceeds as an individual learning experience with the teacher moving about the room from student to student.

**7.3** The teacher states the nature of the learning and focuses upon each student's needs. The lesson is planned as a series of cumulative experiences making use of individual work, group-work and class discussion.

**7.4** The range of cumulative experiences is closely related to the stated objectives behind the lesson. In addition, the teacher manages the learning of students through targeted one-to-one contact which ensures the setting of short- and medium-term goals.

## 8  The relationship to learning in other lessons

**8.1** Although well-planned, the lesson has little to do with previous or future lessons either in style or content.

**8.2** The lesson is part of a sequence of work which is well-understood by the students. Within these lessons, the approach to learning is varied yet teacher expectations are consistent.

**8.3** The lesson is part of a well-developed scheme of work which has been resourced so that individual needs are catered for in a fashion which assures progression and continuity.

**8.4** The lesson is not only well-integrated within a departmental scheme of work but also with cross-curricular approaches. This ensures that work in other curriculum areas is appropriately complemented.

## 9  Teacher-led learning

**9.1** The teacher is the focus of the learning for students. Instruction with little whole class discussion is characteristic. Little attention is paid to encouraging effective or active listening by the students. The teacher rarely changes the tone of delivery and frequently uses inappropriate vocabulary and syntax.

**9.2** More than a third of the lesson is spent on teacher-focused activity. Class discussion predominates with the vast proportion of questions posed by the teacher being closed. Responses by students are usually confined to short answers confirming knowledge recall. Few questions are asked by students.

**9.3** Teacher-focused activity is an important part of the lesson. A clear statement of the lesson's objectives by the teacher at the outset is underpinned by focused discussion at critical points in the lesson. Whilst closed questions are used, the teacher makes conscious use of open questions to encourage an enquiry-based, hypothesis-generating and problem-solving approach.

**9.4** Students' learning is managed in order to make the best use of teacher-focused discussion which arises from individual or collaborative work. As a consequence, a high proportion of students of both sexes is actively engaged in teacher-focused talk in an enquiring environment. Students as well as teachers pose questions in an unthreatening and interested way.

## 10 Student-centred learning

**10.1** Students work on their own from undifferentiated, whole-class material for a large proportion of the lesson. The teacher makes contact with students according to student need; apart from this, little sustained one-to-one contact takes place.

**10.2** Students work from a variety of resources, some of which seek to differentiate the learning experience according to individual needs. The teacher works systematically around the class.

**10.3** Students are guided in their use of particular resources by sensitive curriculum tutoring by the teacher who targets particular students in rotation for sustained support. The teacher keeps good records of student attainment with regular formative profiling at critical points.

**10.4** Flexible learning is understood by all students since it is used consistently across the curriculum. Effective curriculum tutoring means that students are guided to resources and tasks which cater for their individual learning needs and are thus enabled to manage their own learning needs to a considerable extent.

## 11  Study skills

**11.1** Although required to find out for themselves from time to time, students have not been given an appropriate study skills programme and tend to indulge in excessive copying of information when asked to research.

**11.2** All students have received a basic study skills programme which covers access to information, selective reading and note-taking. Little consistent reinforcement of these skills has taken place across the curriculum.

**11.3** Independent study is an integral part of most curriculum areas for all years. Consistent use of study skills is complemented by all teachers through reference to a whole school policy.

**11.4** Study skills across the curriculum are supported by an effective resources centre and the deployment of information technology which assures access to a wide range of information sources which are integrated into the learning experience of students.

## 12  Group-work

**12.1** Group-work is used occasionally. Organisation into groups is haphazard with little attention given to the nature of the group learning experience.

**12.2** Group-work is used frequently but largely for the exercise of functional and prescriptive tasks. Group organisation is seldom reviewed. The nature of group-work and the functions of an effective group are not understood by students.

**12.3** Group-work is used frequently and consistently in all curriculum areas. The make-up of groups is flexible and designed to fit the nature of the learning. Groups understand how to function effectively and are usually constituted in order to perform an open-ended or problem-solving task.

**12.4** Group-work is used as an integral part of all learning experiences and ranges from focused paired talk to large group simulation or problem-solving activities. Students manage themselves well in groups and are able to evaluate their functional effectiveness. The teacher is adept in managing and assessing groups.

## 13 Reading

**13.1** Students are required to read for brief periods of time in order to gain instructions for other activities. Most of their reading is taken from the blackboard or from worksheets.

**13.2** In addition to reading for instructions, students are required to read passages from text-books from time to time; these often have closed answer comprehension questions appended to them.

**13.3** Students are given the opportunity to develop higher order reading skills through the teacher's use of reflective reading strategies. Such occasional *Directed Activities Related to Text* (DARTs) encourage reading for purpose, skimming, scanning, sequencing, prediction and other recreative reading skills.

**13.4** Students frequently use higher order reading skills to aid their studies. The exercise and monitoring of these skills by the teacher has encouraged students to value reading and to make use of the written word in an autonomous way.

## 14 Writing

**14.1** Students' writing is largely concerned with copying and the use of brief answers in response to closed questions.

**14.2** Students are required to write explanations and descriptions of events in a formal way in order that the teacher can check on the subject content that has been taught.

**14.3** In addition to extended formal writing, students are given opportunities to write imaginatively and recreatively. Thus, the transactional and poetic modes of writing are encouraged and assessed by the teacher.

**14.4** Writing is an essential part of the process of learning. Students are encouraged to keep a journal of their learning experiences and to draft responses for their own use which are often shared with the teacher. The teacher encourages the development of this expressive mode into well-constructed and developed transactional and poetic writing. Students are often required to write for audiences other than the teacher.

## 15 Practical work

**15.1** Students are given opportunities occasionally to engage in practical activities. The use of equipment and resources is limited and teacher control of these activities is closely prescribed. Thus, students follow instructions to complete tasks in a functional way.

**15.2** Students are given the opportunity to engage in practical tasks fairly regularly. Most tasks are prescriptively organised by the teacher, however, some involve the exercise of the students' initiative and are somewhat open-ended. The structure for open-ended activity is often too loose and leads to much off-task activity.

**15.3** A wide variety of practical activities takes place. Students understand how to organise themselves and are adept at following instructions as well as addressing problems. The teacher exercises influence over the activities and manages the learning in a sensitive and student-centred way.

**15.4** The teacher is highly skilled at setting practical tasks which enable students to engage with problems in an experimental way. Support is provided and the students understand the structure within which they are operating. The teacher's use of verbal and written questioning is skilful as a way of allowing the students to discover answers for themselves which ensure that learning arises from the practical activities.

## 16  The use of information technology

**16.1** Students receive a basic course in information technology which is rarely complemented within curriculum areas. Occasional use is made of subject-specific software by the subject teacher.

**16.2** The subject teacher is able to make regular use of the school's information technology resources within the classroom. Students use information technology for the development of word processing skills as well as for subject specific learning programs. The teacher relies upon the skills of the school's information technology coordinator.

**16.3** Computers are available in the classroom and are network-linked to the school's information technology centre. The teacher frequently uses the computers to develop skills and experiences for students of all abilities. The commitment to information technology in this curriculum area is clearly stated and contributes to an entitlement provided across the school for all students.

**16.4** The teacher uses computers regularly and confidently as a part of the teaching of all students. Consequently, students are sure of an experience across the curriculum which guarantees competence with word processing, data-bases, spreadsheets and desk-top publishing. Opportunities are found for the use of satellite communication, teletext and other technological information sources.

## 17  Additional classroom support

**17.1** The needs of students with special learning differences are met through extraction from the mainstream classroom. Thus, some students are withdrawn for additional help within the special needs department; this assures some development of basic literacy and numeracy skills.

**17.2** Occasionally, the teacher is supported in the classroom by a special needs teacher. Since this in-class support is intermittent, it is difficult for the two teachers to plan their focus on the particular needs of individual students. The presence of the additional teacher is welcomed by teacher and students.

**17.3** In-class support is a regular feature of classroom management; the intervention is well-planned and the additional teacher's work is targeted flexibly for the benefit of students with particular learning needs. The curriculum area makes use of the special needs coordinator as a consultant who is able to offer advice concerning appropriate methodology and resources.

**17.4** Targeted in-class support is overseen by the consultant coordinator for special educational needs. Individual curriculum areas have named teachers responsible for the management of learning differences. These teachers liaise with the school coordinator and provide guidance in the development of resources and appropriate teaching approaches. Support- and team-teaching take place often and effectively as a result of careful planning and preparation.

## 18  Use of homework

**18.1** Homework is set and marked occasionally and is usually characterised as the continuation of incomplete classwork.

**18.2** Homework is set and marked regularly and frequently; careful teacher assessment helps to differentiate individual student outcomes.

**18.3** The teacher uses homework to reinforce and extend the work of individual students. Tasks and resources are often used which cater for individual needs.

**18.4** Tasks are often set for homework which involve students with an investigative approach to their studies. Thus, autonomous research work and the drafting of ideas are encouraged as ways of supplementing the individualised tasks which are commonly set for homework.

## 19  Monitoring and assessment

**19.1** The teacher marks students' work regularly and provides brief marginalia and summary comment to encourage and guide future work.

**19.2** The teacher keeps a record of the areas for development which are pertinent to individual students; reinforcement and/or extension work is targeted at students which is appropriate to individual needs.

**19.3** The teacher makes use of a system of formative profiling. Students have a clear idea of the general and specific learning objectives behind a unit of work. They are required to reflect upon their progress at significant points and to assess the achievement of their individual targets. The teacher makes contact with individuals on a regular basis in order to assess progress and reinforce or realign targets.

**19.4** The teacher has coordinated the National Curriculum Levels of Attainment with the system of formative profiling. Consequently, assessment procedures are student-centred and diagnostic. Regular feedback to students and their parents ensures short-, medium- and long-term motivation.

### 20  Relevance to National Curriculum Attainment Targets

**20.1** The subject is taught appropriately but with little specific regard to National Curriculum Attainment Targets. The teacher relies upon occasional inputs that are relevant to National Curriculum needs; these are supplemented by summative tests.

**20.2** The teacher works from a well-developed departmental scheme of work which is in accord with National Curriculum Attainment Targets. Lessons are planned according to particular Attainment Targets; students complete standardised tasks to their own level of attainment.

**20.3** The departmental scheme of work provides guidance and support for the teacher and helps ensure that Programmes of Study are taught and assessed. Flexible classroom management means that the teacher is able to cater for individual needs and ensure that work reinforces and extends individual capabilities.

**20.4** The departmental scheme of work relates to similar schemes of work in other curriculum areas. The teacher provides a flexible learning experience which seeks to assess individual student progress formatively and diagnostically. In addition, the teacher complements the work of other curriculum areas. Cross-curricular themes and dimensions are understood by teachers and students in a whole curriculum which does not seek to compartmentalise knowledge, skills, concepts and experience.

# ■ Writing a whole-school 'Teaching and Learning Policy'

The evaluation team took the quality criteria and the action plans of individual faculties and drafted a policy to be agreed and understood by all users – teachers, students and parents. The draft policy was presented to a sample of all users and amended to an acceptably concise and comprehensible form.

# ■ Continued review and evaluation

The policy, together with the quality criteria, were used for faculty review in the way described in Section C2. Individual faculty review statements contributed to the whole school annual review (see Section B6) and enabled the clear setting of priorities for development which were closely allied to resource allocation. The policy statement and the quality criteria were kept under review and amended/extended according to need.

# C2
# Enhancing departmental performance

## ■ Introduction

The headteacher of Abbeydown School was conscious that the work of the school's individual departments was satisfactory, in terms of examination results, but she was by no means certain of the quality of classroom experience and had a limited view of the effectiveness of resource and personnel management in each department.

Every September, she had been in the habit of interviewing each head of department according to a standard agenda:

1   Examination results

2   Implementation of the National Curriculum

3   Staffing

4   Resources

5   Any other business

Whilst she found the discussions open and wide-ranging, she felt that her management of the heads of department could be more systematic and exact. When questioned at a later point in the year, the heads of department stated that they found the senior management team to be remote and unaware of departmental difficulties.

The headteacher determined upon an approach to departmental review which complemented the school's annual review cycle . This, she felt, would add rigour to the process of evaluation and would support and enhance departmental performance.

## ■ The management of departmental review

In May, the headteacher determined that the most effective way of establishing and maintaining close contact with individual departments was by operating a line management structure. Consequently, the senior management team of herself, two deputies and one senior teacher were given responsibility for a range of departments. The four line managers did not have a responsibility for a curriculum area in which they taught.

Responsibilities were divided as follows:

| | |
|---|---|
| Headteacher | *Science and technology* |
| Deputy head 1 | *English, modern languages and mathematics* |
| Deptuy head 2 | *Expressive arts and physical education* |
| Senior teacher | *Humanities and religious education* |

The headteacher stated that she expected the line managers to become au fait with the curriculum and working practices of their nominated departments. This would involve an initial period of familiarisation during which time the line managers would attend departmental meetings, examine departmental documentation, interview the head of department and visit a sample of lessons; in preparation for the new school year.

With the start of the new school year, the senior management team was able to begin its approach to departmental review in earnest. Staff were informed that the new approach was designed to support departments through a more exact understanding of the nature of their work. In addition, heads of department were told that they would not be expected to shoulder a greater burden through this more rigorous evaluation.

Within the first fortnight of the new school year, each head of department met with his/her line manager in order to set the framework and focus for review and development. The first ten weeks of the new year were to be the departmental review weeks which would enable the department to submit its internal review to the senior management team in advance of the whole school review meeting scheduled for the third week in November (see Section B6). The framework for departmental review was established as follows:

1   The department should agree a brief statement concerning its perceived success in respect of the school's aims and derive a set of aims pertinent to the department's practice.

2   The department would agree a number of foci for departmental review with the line manager. These would include scrutiny of examination results.
    For example, the chosen foci for the humanities department were:

- Examination results

- Schemes of work for Key Stage 3 history and geography

- The development of higher order reading skills in history

- The use of information technology in geography

- The post-16 uptake of humanities.

3   The line manager would act as departmental reviewer and would establish agreed approaches to evaluation which would make reasonable use of members of the department and external consultants.

4   The line manager would maintain fortnightly contact with the head of department and regularly attend departmental meetings in order to update on review progress.

5   Three weeks before the end of the departmental review period, the line manager would meet with the head of department to gather information about future staffing and resource needs; these would be an important part of the final review document.

6   The final departmental review document would be written to a common pro-forma (D7) and would inform the departmental review meeting which would be chaired by the line manager in the presence of the department, the headteacher and the governor with nominated responsibility for the department in question.

7   The departmental review meeting would take place at least a week before the whole school review meeting.

8   The departmental review documents would serve as an appendix to the school development plan for the coming year.

## ■ The consequence of departmental review

From the point of view of the headteacher, all departments would receive a focused and pertinent review in the first term of the school year from which priorities for future development would be derived. It would be possible to weigh the priorities for each department against each other and make whole-school decisions which were for the benefit of the students and teachers.

From the teachers' point of view, the senior management team was seen to be more closely involved with departments and more knowledgeable about their problems. Teachers were more assured that priorities were being set for the school on the basis of firm evidence rather than chance views.

Once the review term had finished, departments were in a position to embark upon curriculum and personnel development in preparation for the coming school year. Linking the cycle of review and development to the financial year ensured that the department was able to make best use of time and resources during the school year.

Further review and evaluation took place following the use of a

GRIDS survey (Guidelines for Review and Internal Development of Schools: an approach to school self-evaluation explained in *Reviewing School Departments* SCDC 1989) of departmental concerns in February. Consequently, the line manager was able to mount a further evaluation and development programme through the second half of the school year. In humanities, this led to a consideration of assessment procedures in Years 7 to 11.

The cycle of the departmental year could be summarised in the following way:

| | |
|---|---|
| **September** | Start of new teaching programmes |
| **September to November** | Departmental review |
| **November** | Departmental/school review meetings |
| **February** | Departmental GRIDS survey |
| **April** | Funding for new financial year |
| **April to July** | Evaluation & development programme |
| | Preparation for new school year |

# C3
# Investigating poor examination performance

Shortlisted candidates for the headship of Abbeydown School were sent an analysis of the school's recent examination performance. Governors were clearly disquieted by the school's record, and candidates for final interview were asked to give a presentation to them and their LEA advisers on the school's results, and how they would set about investigating causes and setting in train the means of improvement. The successful candidate gave the following brief introduction to a handout, around which she talked and answered questions.

Whatever reservations we may have about the crudity of examination results as measures of a school's success, it would be foolish to deny their importance to students, parents, employers and teachers alike. All schools have the achievement of academic success and the fulfilment of students' potential as part of their school aims; systematic analysis to ascertain the degree to which these are achieved must therefore take place.

In order to make a realistic assessment of the quality of a set of results, the school must have:

- a standard annual pattern of analysis, compatible with DFE requirements, but which goes into greater detail where needed;

- data on the cohort which enables its performance to be compared with expectations;

- data from schools with which the school is happy to be compared, presented in the same format.

My first concern about Abbeydown's results is that no such systematic analysis, resulting in both a presentation to a governors' meeting and a detailed discussion with each head of department by his or her line manager in the senior management team, seems to take place.

When the assembled array of data indicates concern regarding the performance of a department/faculty, or indeed across the board at A level, the schedule of which I am giving you a copy may be used to address the issue.

The following points are clear about Abbeydown's results; it may be that a great deal more could be said given detailed inside knowledge, but I have exercised caution:

- While the pass rate at A level is satisfactory, being a little above the national average and on or about that for the LEA, the percentage achieving high (C+) grades is alarmingly low. The number of students achieving 20+ higher education points is very small.

- The higher grade (C+) passes at GCSE also make up too low a percentage of the whole; coupled with the very small number achieving 5+ passes at C or above, and the point about A levels, I have a real concern about the degree to which expectations for the more able student are being upheld in the school as a whole.

- On the other hand, the balance of C to D grades at GCSE, the shift in centre of gravity from D to C over the past 3 years, and the consistently high percentage of students achieving 5+ passes at grade G or above, suggests that there are high expectations and a quality programme for those of average and below ability. This is very encouraging, and a springboard from which to work at the more able.

- Why is it that so few students take up geography in the sixth form? The subject produces poor results – is this because only less able students choose it, and is this a result of the options system, or is it some deficiency in the department?

- I would also want to take a hard look at design and technology – results at all levels are mediocre at best.

The handout was as follows:

# INVESTIGATION INTO EXAMINATION RESULTS

1 Before **investigating causes**, review the picture objectively:

- What is the performance by student, grade, subject in relation to other comparable schools over the last 5 years at GC(S)E and A level? (If required, the LEA will help supply data to assist with this analysis.)
- the 'value-added' effect – results at 16 and 18 compared with whatever measure of ability on entry at 11 is available, such as Verbal Reasoning Quotient (VRQ), comparing with other schools where possible.

2 Possible **causes of poor performance** lie in four areas:
   A   the courses
   B   the teaching
   C   the students
   D   the resources

## A: THE COURSES

### A1   Appropriateness
Are the current courses those best suited to the needs of the students and the teachers? Are they attractive, lively and relevant, offering clear progression from previous courses?
*Heads of departments to comment; curriculum deputy to research possible alternatives to 'A' level.*

### A2   Change
Are the courses new, and have changes been accompanied by changes in student performance? Does student performance match prediction?
*Research using school/LEA data.*

### A3   Coherence
Are links between courses sought, and are courses in 'adjacent' curriculum areas compatible?
*Heads of departments to be asked to research.*

## B: THE TEACHING

### B1   Quality
Are teachers qualified and experienced to teach at the required level? Have they a track record of success at this level? Have their skills been enhanced through appropriate staff development?
*Research using school/LEA data.*

### B2   Stability
Have the teachers spent sufficient time at the school to become used to

its practices and to make their full contribution; is there also new blood to refresh the teaching? Are teachers spending excessive amounts of time outside the classroom?
*Research using school/LEA data.*

### B3   Teacher morale
Are teachers confident and generally happy? Do they enjoy teaching in this environment?
*Heads of department to research.*

### B4   Methodology
Are the methods used by teachers appropriate to the needs of the course and the students? Are they varied and lively, offering the opportunity for students to achieve higher order skills such as hypothesis-building, independent research and teamwork? Do teachers adjust their methodologies to take account of the level of independence required by the course of study? Are study skills, independent learning, and responsibility for learning encouraged by teachers, especially by the use of private study time?
*LEA could carry out such a survey.*

### B5   Schemes of work
Are these presented to a common format as a supplement to examination syllabuses? Are they orderly, regularly updated and well-known to the teachers in the department?
*Deputy head to research documents.*

### B6   Assessment
Are students carefully guided through the courses with a full programme of assignments appropriate to the course set and marked? Are students and their parents made fully aware of progress? Are good records kept? Is examination entry policy generous yet realistic, and is exam preparation thorough and professional?
*Heads of departments to be required to conduct surveys.*

### B7   Evaluation
Whose job is it to evaluate teaching in all the ways given above? When was this last carried out and what were the results?

## C  THE STUDENTS

### C1  Guidance
Are students guided into appropriate courses, in terms both of the level of work and the subjects chosen? Is there a prospectus or handbook which assists parents/students in making choices? Whose job is all this and how well is it carried out?
*Survey of student and staff views through questionnaires and interviews.*

**C2  Induction**

Are the students carefully briefed on the demands of the course and introduced to its methods and the group thoughtfully?
*Heads of departments to report on their procedures.*

**C3  Tutoring**

Are the students guided effectively through their courses by tutors who have oversight, through a system of profiling and recording achievement, of their progress?
*LEA survey will provide the basis for a school review.*

**C4  Quality**

Has the ability spread of the students changed markedly and, if so, why?
*Research using school/LEA data.*

**C5  Morale**

Are students happy and settled, enjoying a rich school life? When were they last asked for their views and what were the results?
*see C1*

**D THE RESOURCES**

**D1  Quality**

Are resources supplied in the right numbers, of the right quality, regularly updated, and made available to the students?
*Heads of departments to report, plus an objective survey from a sample of courses.*

**3**  The school should now **decide**:
- whose role it is to manage the investigation;
- since the list above is fairly exhaustive, where the most promising foci might lie;
- the time-scale for the investigations, the task-groups to carry them out, and the dates and methods of reporting;
- the suggested role for the LEA.

# C4
# Improving communications

After six months in post, the headteacher decided to conduct a GRIDS survey to gauge staff views of the school, its management and curriculum. An area that was consistently recorded as an area of weakness was that of communication. Closer scrutiny of the staff opinion questionnaires, backed up by a sample of staff interviews, indicated that the major areas of concern regarding communication were between:

- the senior management team and the staff;
- the school and its partner primary schools;
- the school and the parents.

The headteacher was concerned by these perceived deficiencies and decided to take responsibility herself for a radical review and reshaping of practice.

## ■ Establishing a policy

The headteacher realised that there was a narrow line to tread between too little and too much communication. In her past experience she had heard colleagues criticise senior management because 'they never tell us anything and then make a pretence at consultation' whilst at another school the staff complaint was often – 'I wish they'd do what they're paid for and let us get on with teaching'. She decided that, whilst consultation was her preferred mode, she would adopt a more assertive approach and aim to take the staff with her. Consequently, she wrote a first draft policy statement on communications herself, which she presented to her heads of department. She asked them to consult with their colleagues to refine the principles before submitting the final draft to the governing body for their amendments. In the event, few changes were made during the three stages of consultation and a simple statement of policy was adopted which was written in a way which was acceptable to parents, students and governors.

The unifying principle was simple –

> **Abbeydown School aims to keep all members of its community informed on a regular basis and to involve them, as appropriate, with the decisions that are likely to directly affect them.**

Of equal importance was the commitment to keep communications direct, open and straightforward.

## ■ Implementing the policy

In order to achieve this aim, the headteacher called an extended senior management team meeting to draw up a draft implementation plan with which to support the communication policy. The senior management team asked themselves a series of simple questions to which, initially, they brainstormed responses before determining on the structure of meetings and consultations to supplement the style implicit in the communications policy.

1  **What channels of communication need to exist internally between:**

- SMT and the staff as a whole
- SMT and the department heads
- SMT and the pastoral team
- SMT and students
- the pastoral team and form tutors
- members of departments
- the teaching staff and the ancillary teams
- the staff and the governing body?

2  **What channels of communication does the school need to exist externally with:**

- the students' parents
- the partner primary schools
- other tertiary providers
- the careers service
- the Local Education Authority
- the local business community
- the local community?

3  **Does a named member of staff have responsibility for any of these channels of communication?**
   The response to this question was relatively unanimously 'not as such', apart from four areas:

- the headteacher in respect of the governing body;
- the head of Year 7 in respect of partner schools;
- the head of careers in respect of the careers service;
- the head of sixth form in respect of tertiary colleges.

**4    Do we need to make certain staff responsible for functions that are currently lacking?**

Some responsibilities were determined and written into the job descriptions of members of the senior management team. Others were recommended to the governing body as appointments to be supported in a phased way as funds permitted:

- responsible for ancillary staff (deputy head 1)

- the school council (senior teacher)

- Education: industry links

- Publicity in the local community

**5    Do we have an adequate meetings' structure to service these communication channels?**

The senior management team were anxious to ensure coverage without overload since they were well aware that nothing was more irritating to staff, in particular, than 'yet another meeting where nothing is achieved'. As a consequence it was decided to determine and post the meeting structure with some underlying principles for effective meeting management.

The following meetings were scheduled to incorporate those which were already established and deemed to be effective:

- a termly full governors' meeting

- regular governor sub-committee meetings: Finance; Personnel; Curriculum

- a weekly senior management team meeting

- a morning staff briefing

- a monthly full staff meeting

- a monthly heads of department meeting

- a monthly report of student assessment

- a half-termly year meeting to review student assessments

- a monthly meeting of the school council (representatives of the student body)

- a twice-yearly consultation evening with all parents

- a half-termly meeting with partner schools

- a half-termly meeting with tertiary colleges

- a schedule of regular contacts with local employers.

The following principles were established for all meetings:

**(a)** Full agendas should be posted in advance.

**(b)** Minutes should be taken (preferably by secretarial staff).

**(c)** Action points should be attributed and dated.

**(d)** All parties present should be encouraged to contribute.

**(e)** All contributors should be listened to.

**(f)** Chairpersons should ensure:

- that one person speaks at a time;
- contributions are heard to their conclusion;
- outcomes are confirmed;
- meetings keep to time.

**(g)** All meetings should aim to be open, honest, supportive and productive.

6    **Do we need to improve our written communications?**
The overwhelming 'Yes' response to this question led the senior management team to recommend certain specific recommendations:

- an upgrading of the school's prospectus

- a review of the staff handbook

- an improvement to notice-boards in the staffroom and around the school

- a review of the procedure and presentation of internal communication to staff

- a commitment to face-to-face communication in preference to written communication, where possible

- an improvement in the letter-head and quality of typeface on letters leaving school

- a survey of the letters sent to parents in terms of quantity and quality

- the creation of a monthly newsletter to parents

- the creation of a weekly internal broadsheet for staff and students

- a review of the termly school magazine

- a commitment to regular features about the school in local media.

7   **What can we do to supplement the school communication style?**
The senior management team decided that accessibility and visibility were the essential ingredients of success in response to this question. Consequently, they became committed to maintaining a presence around the school in corridors, classrooms and the staffroom in which they sought to speak to students and staff in an open, direct, honest and interested way. In addition, they determined to attend those meetings where their presence would be valued.

8   **How will we know when we have improved our channels of communication?**
All members of the senior management team agreed that there was one simple answer –

'By asking people how we are doing'.

# C5
# Improving budget management

The finance sub-committee of the governing body of Abbeydown School was alarmed at the apparent lack of any system for budget management in the school. The sub-committee had been called into being in the last year of the previous headship, as a result of the chairman's attendance at a governor training session during which the value of such a group was emphasised by many of those present. One of the main reasons for the previous head's slightly early retirement had been his distaste for the greater emphasis on resource management which LMS brought to his role, and the decision-making and accountability which went with it.

Very early in her headship, the governors asked the new head to draft for them a system of budget management and monitoring for the school. The precise brief was to produce recommendations for

- an annual budget planning cycle;
- the roles of those individuals and groups with budget responsibilities;

- criteria for budget allocation;
- the means of regular monitoring of the budget.

The head (who had arrived in January) asked for the remainder of the school year to see present practice through, and to get to know the LEA personnel and systems. The following is the paper she presented to the full governing body in July of her first year.

'The school's finances have always been managed with scrupulous care and honesty. In trying to update the financial systems to take account of the needs facing the school now, I have become aware of the following development needs:

- The school has traditionally handled different pockets of money (such as staffing budgets, PTA funds and 'capitation') separately; we now need to take a wider view of resources and of support to the school.
- The budget has been allocated to 'spending departments' on historic criteria, rather than on the needs expressed in the development plan; the budget must henceforth be seen as the short term means of achieving our development priorities.
- Rather than a single sum to each 'spending department', the budget now needs to contain maintenance and development components. Each department should receive an amount to maintain itself with consumables etc.; the development plan priorities will then determine where the remaining fraction will be spent, and in roughly what proportion.
- In principle, I would like the school to move over time towards LMS for departments, so that faculty/department heads have some choice – between equipment and secretarial support, for example. Each middle manager would therefore become a resource centre manager.
- The school has also been reactive, rather than trying to plan ahead; I want the culture of the school to be based on self-evaluation and planning, leading to ownership and autonomy.
- As a longer-term strategy, but to begin immediately, the school must consider the income side of its budget. This includes minor points such as lettings, and linking PTA funds into the whole and not considering them necessarily as separate pots of money, even though they may require separate accounting. Principally, however, it means vigorous attention to future numbers in the school, particularly to recruitment at Y7 and 12, and therefore to marketing (see C6)

Finally in this introduction I would say that, important as money is to making the school operate, I will not let it dominate other, more important, issues. We have a good bursar and office staff to run all the details – I do not want myself, my senior management team colleagues and the governors bogged down in pence or in budget tabulations and minutiae. We are here to take a broad view, and to take decisions which help teachers do a more effective job with young people.

It is against these general principles that I present my proposals under the four headings requested by governors:

## 1   Annual budget cycle

As stated above, the budget planning cycle is intimately tied in to the development and review cycle; in the table which follows, I have kept strictly to budget processes and events, but governors should be aware of a much more detailed year plan which weaves around this one:

| | |
|---|---|
| *April* | beginning of financial year<br>funds available to departments to spend |
| *May* | finalisation of out-turn of last year's budget (or June) |
| *June* | presentation of final accounts from last year to governors, staff |
| *July* | ditto to parents at AGM |
| | first quarterly check on spending; finance sub-committee to consider |
| *August* | |
| *Sept* | |
| *Oct* | second quarterly check on spending; finance sub-committee to consider receipt of comparative data from LEA on spending profiles of other schools<br>first major look at next financial year – number on roll, staff costs etc |
| *Nov* | (Annual Curriculum Review) |
| *Dec* | (Begin to redraft school development plan) |
| *Jan* | third quarterly check on spending; supplementary estimates if possible; senior management team and governors' finance sub-committee consider final draft budget |
| *Feb* | final budget figures confirmed by LEA publication of final budget to governors, staff |
| *Mar* | year end check and statement; departmental allowances published |
| *April* | beginning of financial year; funds available to departments to spend |

## 2   Roles of those concerned with budget

At present, these are not clear, and should be formalised as soon as possible. I present the following proposal as a first draft:

Bursar (and office staff)
- raises orders and maintains computer records
- produces statements and summaries for governors quarterly (and as required), and for head and budget holders monthly
- alerts headteacher to trends and potential problems in the budget
- works regularly with LEA finance officer for both training and consultancy.

Since the bursar is in charge of the non-teaching staff, and since her knowledge of finance will be invaluable to its discussions, I want her to attend heads of department (Academic Board) meetings from September; she will also attend key budget meetings of the senior management team and will often be invited to finance sub-committee meetings.

Headteacher (and senior management team)
- is updated regularly on budget position and approves minor adjustments
- prepares a draft budget for governors
- prepares policy options when budget changes are necessary, evaluates them in the light of the school development plan and makes recommendations to governors
- communicates issues and needs to the LEA, partly through meetings with its finance officer

Governors (finance sub-committee):
- receives the reports and recommendations of the headteacher
- makes decisions to be ratified by the full governing body.

## 3   Criteria for budget allocation

As I stated in my introduction, budgets to 'departments' (I will prefer the term resource centre managers) will be allocated according to two criteria:
- a formula for the basic or maintenance budget, based on the number of pupil periods taught by the department, plus a factor for how expensive in consumables or equipment the department is;
- a development budget based on the priorities expressed in the school development plan.

Resource centre managers will be responsible to their line manager within the senior management team for monitoring and spending their budget, and will be given monthly updates on the state of those budgets by the bursar's office.

The school will aim to have a 2% contingency fund.

## 4    Means of regular budget monitoring

The IT equipment in our office allows accurate and regular monitoring.

As section (2) on responsibilities stated, the bursar's office will be responsible for producing summaries and statements monthly for myself and all budget holders, for each meeting of the finance sub-committee, and quarterly for governors. These summaries will normally be set out in the headings below (For each heading there would be a figure for amount allocated and % committed.):

Teaching staff

Maintenance

Supply teaching

Energy

Non-teaching staff

Water/other utilities

Advertising/Interview

Sub-total: Premises-related

Sub-total: Staffing related expenditure

expenditure

Sub-total: Transport-related expenditure

Sub-total: Administration-related expenditure

Sub-total: Pupil-related expenditure

We have developed a financial year profile. Given salary increase and incremental points, the percentage of the fuel bill we expect to incur quarterly, and the times in the year when books and equipment are bought, we expect to spend the following % of our budget by the end of the month shown:

April: 7%     July:    35%    Oct:  58%    Jan: 82%
May: 16%     August: 43%    Nov:  66%    Feb: 90%
June: 26%    Sep:     50%    Dec:  75%    Mar: 98%

All Academic Board meetings will have an agenda item for the bursar to update, and members to question, on the state of the budget. At each summer term meeting of the governors, the headteacher will present a summary of the out-turn against predicted budget. Governors will present a similar item to parents at their AGM.

Any significant departures from budget will be dealt with as follows:

1    Potential underspends will be the subject of supplementary estimates, normally following the third quarterly budget check in February. Such estimates from resource centre managers will be summarised and evaluated by senior management team, with recommendations, for the finance sub-committee. Or it may be decided to roll the money forward to the next financial year, either because a large project is high on the school development plan agenda, or because financial stringency looms.

2    Potential overspends will be picked up by the monthly monitoring of overall percentage and category. Small changes may be made by the head, using contingency or underspends from other headings, and informed to the next finance sub-committee meeting. More major issues must be raised at the sub-committee, which will normally require the head to present to the next meeting a number of options for rectifying the situation, with an evaluation of their impact, and a recommendation.

# C6
# Preparing a marketing plan

## Introduction

As much as the realisation pained her, the headteacher of Abbeydown School recognised that the school existed in a competitive climate. With The Ragged Mount School two miles away and a declining student population in the locality, she knew that the school must market itself in order to gain a reasonable slice of available resources. Mercifully, a code of conduct had been established by the LEA which had maintained civilised practices and working relationships between secondary schools since the 1986 and 1988 Acts. However, the prospect of The Ragged Mount School assuming grant-maintained status caused the headteacher at Abbeydown to view the future with caution.

External problems were exacerbated by the recession of the early 1990s which discouraged local businesses (notwithstanding the work of the Education: Business Partnership) from taking an active interest in the school and its leavers. Internal problems did not make the head's task of marketing the school any easier. The spectre of staff redundancies made it difficult for a certain proportion of staff to accept expenditure on marketing strategies when the curriculum was under threat. The headteacher knew that a marketing plan was highly desirable and that the management of it would be one of her most challenging tasks.

## Raising awareness

In line with her commitment to open management, the headteacher, with a member of the governors' finance sub-committee, presented a picture of the global budget to the staff at the full staff meeting in October. She chose this point in the year since it coincided with preparation of the development plan and was sufficiently distant from the time when the coming year's budget would need to be set. She presented an outline of the previous year's income and expenditure, placing emphasis upon the main sources of revenue against the major staffing and premises costs.

She was able to present some illustrative performance data concerning the previous budget to aid staff understanding of the use of resources and its cost effectiveness. Thus, staff were helped to recognise:

- the revenue provided by each student in Key Stages 3 to 5;
- the staffing allocation for each year group;
- the average cost of a lesson;
- the expenditure on classroom resources per student;
- the implications of lost student numbers in each of these respects.

The LEA was able to offer county average comparative data to show the cost effectiveness of Abbeydown School.

Having raised staff awareness about the budget and its implications, the headteacher turned attention away from these matters and emphasised the strengths and qualities of the school. She was able to take the current, annual evaluation of aims (see Section B2) and celebrate the successes which were apparent to staff, students and the wider community. She stressed that continued success and development depended upon maintaining student numbers and a positive attitude towards the school in the local community. At this point, she felt it was possible to broach the subject of marketing and the need for a plan with the caveat that this did not mean vigorous offers of free gifts or other spurious incentives to students and parents. Some staff felt that such an approach was against the spirit of the education service that they had joined; the majority, however, were prepared to acknowledge the need for sensitive marketing.

# ■ Marketing principles

The essential marketing ingredient, as far as the headteacher of Abbeydown School was concerned, was **quality**. It was her intention to ensure that the school provided a distinctive education for its students within the framework of the National Curriculum. She was committed to the maintenance of quality and the communication of that quality to all partners. In other words, her basic marketing principle was that the school should emphasise the **benefits** to the local community of an education for young people at Abbeydown School.

These benefits needed to be stated clearly, concisely and in a language that could be understood by all users. The unifying school aim was, thus, central to her marketing purpose. She baulked at calling this aim a 'mission statement' but was steadfast in the belief that it was the only way of ensuring unity of purpose. Thus the adapted aim became:

> **Abbeydown School provides its students with a stimulating and enjoyable curriculum which is relevant to their individual needs and which enables them to make the most of their abilities.**

In the light of this aim, it became desirable to examine the ingredients that would ensure that this positive image could be substantiated in reality. The simplistic 'product' of Abbeydown was readily identifiable: well-adjusted and flexible young people who were qualified through their education to take those opportunities that would guarantee them personal satisfaction and social usefulness. However, the 'product' of Abbeydown School was more various than this simple and, in any event, elusive notion.

The quality of the school was manifest in a number of ways, all of which contributed to the simple output summarised above. The headteacher felt that quality should be apparent in the following contributory areas of the school:

- the varied and relevant way in which teachers taught;

- the ways in which success was recognised and student improvement assured;

- the additional activities that were provided for students beyond the National Curriculum requirements;

- the demeanour, attitudes and professionalism of teachers and ancillary staff;

- the attitudes of students to each other, their teachers, their school and their education;

- the way in which the school communicated with its partners – be they parents, other educational providers, members of local industry or the wider community;

- the appearance of the school as a calm, orderly and vibrant learning environment;

- the resources available for the students' educational fulfilment; and many more.

Thus, within the development planning cycle, the headteacher sought to gather the information which would indicate that quality was being achieved at Abbeydown School. Once she had a clear notion of the quality within the school she was in a position to market the benefits to parents and the local community of Abbeydown School.

The headteacher determined upon the following checklist of questions to inform her marketing strategies:

1   What makes Abbeydown School special?

2   What are we trying to market as the product of Abbeydown School?

3 How is this product manifest to those within the school?

4 How are we viewed in the wider community?

5 How can we communicate our product to those outside the school?

6 How can we encourage those outside the school to recognise our quality?

7 In what ways do we need to improve our provision in order to enhance ourselves?

## ■ Marketing information

In order to begin to answer these questions, the headteacher realised that she needed to gather and interrogate a variety of information that would enable her to have an objective view of the school. Such a task fitted comfortably into the development planning cycle; she was anxious to prove to staff that marketing was no more than a natural part of their coherent approach to school development. Much information was readily available from the LEA and included the following:

- the projected demographic figures;

- the destinations of Year 6 students in the locality;

- the destinations and achievements of past students;

- comparative data with other schools in respect of –
  entry qualifications of students
  absence rates
  exclusion rates
  examination performance
  the responsibility, age and sex profile of staff
  deployment of budget.

Such data was invaluable for the headteacher in order to help her to answer the basic questions: 'How are we doing?' and 'How might we improve?' She was determined not to use the data to score points off other schools or to cause her to change the nature of the school and the function it served in the local community. She was aware of schools that had misappropriated notions of marketing and sought to change the nature of their intake in order to enhance their simplistic conception of 'product'.

In addition to this information, the headteacher decided to indulge in some limited market research. She sought to see how the school was viewed by parents, local partner schools and the business community. However, she was conscious of the dangerous pitfall of asking too many people too many questions; this might persuade them that she lacked confidence in what Abbeydown was providing (see Section B8).

Her marketing research was simple and centred upon two questions:

- How well do we communicate?

- How well do we listen?

She posed these questions informally but systematically to certain individuals in the local community and formally via a detailed but straightforward questionnaire to the Year 8 parents. The results of this analysis of information together with the internal development plan audit were combined and presented as a basis for producing a marketing plan.

## ■ The marketing cycle

A governors' marketing sub-committee was constituted with the initial brief of producing a plan for the coming year and a way of tying the marketing cycle to the development plan cycle. The outline marketing plan that arose from the analysis of information had two parts:

1   Internal developments

2   External developments.

Both were fundamentally concerned with the optimum deployment of resources to the end of assuring quality provision for the students in the school. **Internal developments** were concerned with ways of improving the quality of the curriculum, the deployment of teachers, the environment, resources for learning and the satisfaction of students. **External developments** were largely concerned with improving the quality of communications and relationships with partners such as parents and the local community. Some examples from each of these categories are provided below as **marketing strategies**.

The marketing cycle that was determined followed the cycle of the school's development plan. The targets for the first year were set in train from April. They were evaluated as they were established in order that a costed review and future plan for marketing action could be examined as a substantive agenda item at the school's annual review meeting in November. The budget for discrete marketing strategies was set at the end of the whole school review procedure so that future action and evaluation could be committed for the start of the next financial year.

# ■ Marketing strategies

The following strategies were adopted in the first year's marketing plan for Abbeydown School. All strategies need to be seen in the context of budgetary constraints and a commitment to maintain quality in accord with the unifying aim of the school.

**Internal developments**

1   Maintenance of the provision for special educational needs

2   Provision of an 'A' allowance and appropriate resources to support the development of flexible learning

3   Enhancement of information technology in key curriculum areas

4   Refurbishment of staff study and resources area

5   Staff development for office reception staff

6   Improvement of school entrance and signs about the school

7   Posting of school aim in all classrooms, foyer, staffroom and offices

8   Employment of part-time handyman to begin rolling programme of environmental improvement

**External developments**

1   Review of school communication with the wider community – including the prospectus, letter-heads, written style and readability

2   Development of curricular links with partner primary schools

3   Launch of post-16 'Challenge of Industry' conference with local business community

4   Regular presentation of the school's achievements in the local press

5   Survey of parental satisfaction with Years 7 and 11

**Future priorities**

1   Maintain a resource and staffing allocation which permits teachers to deliver the school's aim of catering for the needs of individuals

2   Seek opportunities to open the school more widely to the local community; acquire community status and employ a full-time community warden

3   Refurbish the entrance foyer

4   Improve the quality of display boards around the school

5   Establish a programme of environmental improvement which is clear to all teachers

6   Produce a new school brochure and promotional video

7   Foster a sense in all parties of 'What makes Abbeydown School special?'

8   Designate a member of staff to act as marketing manager.

## ■ The quality circle and the seal of approval:

When offered the opportunity to pursue British Standards accreditation or Total Quality Management, the headteacher of Abbeydown School was adamant –

> 'I am anxious that we invest as much as possible of *our* available time and resources in *our* system to examine *our* practice in the light of *our* plan. We will not allow ourselves to be seduced into approaches which distract us from our central purpose of providing a quality education for all our students. I believe that we are good and that we provide a quality service to the local community. I think we should be proud of ourselves and not afraid to tell others about the work we do and what all of our students achieve. There are areas in which we can and must improve. I want us to be brave enough to accept criticism and to address those areas where our quality falls below acceptable standards.'

As a consequence, the school produced its quality summary at the end of each year's review cycle. This amounted to a simple statement of areas of school performance where quality had been achieved and areas where improvements needed to be made. In addition, Year 11 and 13 students were provided with a list of aspects of school performance which were considered to be indicators of quality in respect of the unifying aim. They were asked to grade the school on a four-point impression scale.

At the end of this process, the school was able to award its own seal of approval and give evidence to its community and partners of its unique qualities and areas for improvement. If it were anxious to gain an external seal of approval it could seek a Parents' Charter Mark or the School's Curriculum Award.

## C7
# Monitoring whole- and cross-curricular themes

## ■ Managing the curriculum as a whole

The National Curriculum was conceived as a collection of discrete subjects each with its own Attainment Targets and Programmes of Study. This left considerable room for manoeuvre on the part of individual teaching departments to devise their own schemes of work and styles of teaching. Because of the subject specific orientation of the National Curriculum, it has been rather more difficult for schools to manage the curriculum as a whole and to provide a complementary experience for students. Despite the encouragement of the National Curriculum Council, it has been difficult for managers to break the rapidly cast mould of ten subjects plus religious education.

In primary schools, it has been necessary to retain a more holistic approach to the planning and delivery of the curriculum. This is the result of the scale of many of these schools and the proven success, in some areas, of an integrated approach to teaching. The majority of primary schools have nominated coordinators for specific subjects in the National Curriculum who have provided guidance in the implementation of sometimes demanding programmes of study. In some schools there has been a movement away from the 'integrated day' towards the provision of some subject specific 'lessons'. Despite this, young people in Year 6 still receive a more integrated experience than that which is generally available in Year 7; their first year in secondary education.

Without doubt, most students welcome the change of regime from primary into secondary; they are ready for a change. However, many headteachers and curriculum managers in secondary schools believe that the transition could be more gradual, that the secondary curriculum has much to learn from the primary experience and that a more complementary and coherent experience could be made available within the confines of the National Curriculum, notwithstanding the move towards subject specific teaching in Years 5 and 6. With this view in mind, many schools have appointed two senior staff as coordinators of Key Stage 3 and Key Stage 4. Their job descriptions are largely committed to weaving together the subject-oriented curriculum and ensuring that students experience progression from past achievement towards the realisation of their potential.

As with many aspects of current school management, the starting point is often an audit of current practice and experience. This is followed by the drawing up of a curriculum map. In simple terms this amounts to answering the following questions:

1   What have students experienced in the past?

2   What are we doing now?

3   Who does what at the moment?

4   What else do we want to provide?

5   What else are we required to provide?

6   How can we make it all fit?

Approaches differ, the following are a range of strategies that have been employed.

## ■ Content shared is content halved

At the very simplest level, curriculum mapping can work when the Programmes of Study for particular subjects are seen to be a part of the curriculum in another area. Thus, there has been a very rapid trade off between geography and science departments in schools over the earth science Attainment Targets. Since geography have always taught the content, why should science have to start? The initial role of the key stage coordinators is to ensure adequate coverage between the two discrete departments. Beyond this, the coordinator can help match the curriculum so that complementary teaching can take place in science and geography at appropriate points; the goal is progression and not repetition.

Such curriculum monitoring can be managed in respect of aspects of teaching which are common to a number of schemes of work. For example, the use of graphs may be in the attainment targets and programmes of study for mathematics and science but it is an integral part of the work of geography, history, design and technology and English. It is, therefore, desirable that the teaching of these skills is consistent across the curriculum and, as before, presented at an appropriate time to ensure proper progression.

Since the Key Stage 3 coordinator's role is concerned with the mapping of progression routes, s/he must spend time liaising with Key Stage 2 partners as well as ensuring that skills, experiences and concepts progress through the secondary years.

## ■ Managing a cross-curricular theme

There are, of course, aspects of a student's education which are not the province of a single curriculum area. Many of these have been delineated by the National Curriculum Council and include health education, economic and industrial understanding and careers education. It is perfectly possible for these, themes to be taught as discrete modules; but their full applications are unlikely to be realised if this is the sole means of delivery. More sensible is the curriculum audit and mapping suggested by the questions posed above.

In one school, an audit of health education took place. In the first instance, a long list was established which described the aspects of health education that were considered to be essential to a student's secondary education. A grid was assembled which summarised where these various aspects of health education were currently taking place in Years 7 to 11. The Key Stage coordinators then surveyed the provision through interviews with staff, questionnaires to students, scrutiny of schemes of work and observation of lessons. As a result, a report was written which summarised the current curricular provision, the gaps and repetitions that existed, the progression routes that needed developing and the resource provision that would be required to ensure an acceptable programme for health education. Individual departments were required to commit parts of their schemes of work to aspects of health education which would lead to a coherent, complementary and responsible provision for all students. For example, the English department developed a literature-based module on the issue of abortion and guaranteed to invite external speakers to visit to talk to all Year 10 students. The PE and science departments combined to complement each other's work concerning health-related fitness in Years 7 and 8. The design and technology faculty committed time to health and safety issues to coincide with the history department's unit of work on the industrial revolution.

In another school, the statutory requirements for information technology were managed across the curriculum in a similar fashion. The school had a well-established modular course in Year 7 and an accredited opportunity for students in Year 12. However, there were limited opportunities for students to use information technology as a part of their whole curriculum. Given the provision of adequate resources in most curriculum areas, departments were asked to commit themselves to modules of work which lent themselves to the use of information technology:

- All students were expected to word process a piece of work for English and history in each of the terms of Key Stage 3.

- The compilation and interrogation of data-bases became an integral part of work in science and geography.

- Spread-sheets were introduced and regularly used in mathematics.

- Computer-assisted design was available for all students in Year 9 and thereafter in design and technology.

- The art and English departments sought to develop desk-top publishing in Key Stage 3.

- The music department exploited the opportunities provided by keyboards.

- The drama department introduced GCSE students to computerised lighting and sound effects.

In other words, all areas of the curriculum were committed to regular use of information technology in a way which would assure the experience for all students. It was the job of the key stage coordinators to ensure that adequate coverage was maintained and that progression ensued.

## Assuring a consistent approach

It is one thing to draw up a curriculum map; it is quite another to ensure consistency of approach. A more difficult role for some key stage coordinators has been the management of cross-curricular dimensions like equal opportunities and teaching and learning styles. The management of equal opportunities at Abbeydown School is described in section C8.

In yet another school, the key stage coordinators were charged with the job of monitoring the styles of teaching and learning so that the school management could be confident that students experienced a varied yet complementary diet from their teachers. This involved survey work based upon the statements to be found in the school's 'Teaching and learning policy' and 'Assessment policy'. As a result of an evaluation programme, which culminated in the matching of evidence to the quality criteria (see Sections C2 and D3), the coordinators were able to give notice of areas for improvement which were woven into the school development plan.

## An integrated approach to Year 7

A few schools have responded radically to the National Curriculum and tried to provide continuity of experience from Key Stage 2 to Key Stage 3.

In these cases, areas of the curriculum have been integrated so that students are taught by fewer teachers who teach across a number of National Curriculum subjects. Such an approach requires a blocked timetable so that teams of teachers can work together to offer subject-specific expertise, team teach or exchange classes to cover areas of specialism.

The Year 7 model operating in one school led to each class being taught by six teachers at any one time over a 25 period week:

| | |
|---|---|
| English, humanities and religious education | 8 periods |
| Science and mathematics | 6 periods |
| Design and technology | 3 periods |
| Expressive arts | 3 periods |
| Modern languages | 3 periods |
| Physical education | 2 periods |

Personal and social education is mapped across the curriculum and focused by each class tutor, who also teaches one of the curriculum areas.

The advantages of coherence arise from teachers working in teams and sharing expertise for course planning and delivery. In this model teachers are concerned with the consistent management of their students' learning. Opportunities for formative assessment within a differentiated curriculum are abundant. The model depends upon capable and flexible teachers; one poor or uncommitted teacher can damage the education of a large proportion of students. In some schools this integrated experience has been maintained in part throughout Key Stage 3.

## ■ Focus experiences in Key Stage 4

Some schools have taken the opportunity to focus the curriculum through specific events which draw upon all curriculum areas. An obvious example is the use of work experience, when all students in Years 10 or 11 are taken off timetable for a week. At best, work experience is tied to the curriculum so that students are placed in a relevant place of employment from which they can derive experience which relates to an area of study. For example, a female student in one school used her experience in a local planning department to further a special study in geography; a male student visited a French school as a teacher's assistant; whilst elsewhere a Year 10 class were required to write up their experiences as a piece of GCSE English coursework.

The residential experience, which takes students off timetable and places them in a different environment where they are required to exercise a wide variety of skills from the physical and personal to the problem-solving and social, has a similarly coherent educational effect.

Many schools take a theme for a week or a day and focus the work of all departments on it. For example, one school devoted a week to economic and industrial understanding for all Year 9 students. Departments provided inputs to an off-timetable week which gave students some very diverse but relevant experiences. The success of this particular enterprise lay in the fact that each class was required to make a presentation at the end of the week to chart their understanding and involvement with the work in question.

All of the examples quoted above are isolated. No school has managed to respond to the National Curriculum with an exhaustive map which ensures a totally coherent experience for all students. The least success-ful schools are those which take a list of cross-curricular themes and try to tick them off year-by-year. Such an approach is rarely developmental and does little to suggest coherence to teachers and their students. The best examples are from schools that have decided to start in a small way, experiment, make mistakes and continue to roll ideas forward. In these schools the key stage coordinator has a crucial  managerial role in ensur-ing that contracted work is undertaken within the schemes of work of individual departments.

# C8
# Enhancing equal opportunities

Whereas a commitment to equal opportunities at Abbeydown School was espoused in the school's basic aim, the headteacher felt that there was a disturbing gap between rhetoric and reality. The principal commitment: 'To cater for all individuals according to their needs and so ensure that their potentials are realised', was not as apparent in reality as, she per-ceived, it might be. The following evidence was readily available:

GCSE examination performance by male students was considerably worse than that of female students and yet abilities on entry were almost exactly comparable.

|  | M | F |
|---|---|---|
| Average VRQ on Y7 entry | 94.5 | 95.2 |
| % in lowest VRQ quintile | 22.3% | 23.1% |
| Average reading age on Y7 entry | 10.8 | 11.2 |
| % achieving 5 + GCSE A–C | 23% | 37% |
| % leaving with no GCSE A–G | 5.6% | 1.3% |

Some interesting data had emerged following a number of student pursuits, which had been undertaken in the previous school year by way of monitoring and improving the effectiveness of teaching and learning (see Section C1).

During classroom discussion in most of the secondary years, male students had dominated the responses to teacher and were felt by many observers to 'create the tone in lessons'. Some experiments had been undertaken in respect of mixed and single-sex groupings for enquiry-based work by a teacher in the humanities faculty by way of action research (see Section D7), which showed a marked difference in performance depending upon group structure.

Difficulties had arisen for the head of lower school through a spate of inadequate homework by a large number of boys in Y8.

Although Abbeydown School had few students from ethnic minority backgrounds, a number of racist comments were beginning to be apparent to several teachers of classes in Key Stage 3.

Taken separately, much of this data could be overlooked. However, taken as a whole, the headteacher felt that some concerted action needed to be taken in respect of equal opportunities. She was aware that the issue would be a potential minefield. Several staff had expressed sceptical views about equal opportunities. They felt that good practice was 'implicit in all we do' and that undue attention would create a problem where one did not particularly exist. Such a view was prevalent amongst many members of the governing body. It was clear that she would have to take staff with her and that a planned and long-term approach would be the one most likely to win hearts and minds.

## ■ Problem, what problem?

The headteacher began by confirming her own discomfort about equal opportunities at Abbeydown School by reference to hard data. She felt convinced that the only way to challenge the attitudes of her colleagues was through the presentation of a critical assessment of the school's performance in respect to equal opportunities. She felt that she had the ideal leader for such a base-line survey in her most recently appointed deputy. As a senior member of staff who had been in post for six months, he had the necessary objectivity to present an 'outsider's' view of the school.

The new deputy was, therefore, charged with the task of gathering as much information as was currently available regarding of equal opportunities at Abbeydown. He set himself a month to gather the data, at which point he was to present his critique to a full staff meeting and, subsequently, to the governing body.

Much data was readily available; he focused on the following evidence from the previous five years and concentated attention upon the relevant performance of male and female students and the performance of students from ethnic minority backgrounds.

- Y7 VRQ data

- Y7 Reading ages and other internal screening data

- GCSE results in core subjects

- GCSE optional choices

- First destinations of students at 16+

- Destinations of students at 18+

- A training and employment profile, to date, of the cohort of students from five years ago

- Provision of educational support to statemented students

- Provision and type of support teaching to individual curriculum areas

- Summary observations from sample students pursuits

- Distribution of posts of responsibility within the staff.

Following his presentation of data, the following summary points were made in respect of Abbeydown School as a provider of Equal Opportunities

1  Males were underperforming females significantly in GCSE examinations

2  Females were underperforming in science against their mean performance at GCSE

3   Females and males were choosing GCSE options in a stereotypical fashion

4   Vocational choices post-16 showed an even distribution by the sexes into business and finance, an upward trend of males into the 'female' province of catering and a majority of females in service and caring courses

5   'A' level choices showed a larger uptake by males in mathematics and the sciences (with the exception of biology). There was an even distribution into the humanities with more females choosing English, art-related subjects and theatre studies.

6   Over five years, 41% of students continued on to higher education. Of these, 65% were male and 35% female. The majority of males followed courses in science, engineering, business, law or finance. The majority of females followed courses in the arts, humanities and teaching. Over the past five years, three female students had followed courses in engineering and medicine, whilst 15 male students had done so.

7   Although there were more females of lower ability in the student population over the past five years, more males had left school at 16 without any qualifications.

8   The school's commitment to in-class support teaching had meant in practice that one lesson in 19 had in-class support in Key Stage 3 and one lesson in 32 in Key Stage 4.

9   Although concerned to develop differentiated approaches to learning, few departments had resources or timetable provision to facilitate this.

10  Males were regarded as 'establishing the tone' in most lessons.

11  For the first time, two cases of racial harassment had been reported in the last year. Teachers were evenly divided in their views that racism is no problem here and 'racism is part of the culture of our students'.

12  The majority of responsibility posts on the staff were occupied by male teachers. Female heads of department were in post in English, mathematics, home economics, learning support and physical education.

## ■ Action, what action?

Heated discussions at staff level resulted in polarised positions between those who felt that 'we can't be expected to solve society's problems' and those who felt that 'the school has a case to answer'.

The headteacher determined upon a course of positive action:

1   An 'Equal opportunities' working party should be constituted under the deputy head who had undertaken the initial survey, with representation from a member of the Governing Body;

2   The working party should be charged to gather any further information over contentious issues and draft an equal opportunities policy for the school;

3   Once the policy had been accepted by staff and governors, the working party should draft a positive action plan in respect of equal opportunities;

4   Each department should be required to report on action in respect of equal opportunities as a part of their annual review;

5   The school should be required to report on action in respect of equal opportunities within its development plan and annual review meeting.

After a similarly heated discussion at the governors' meeting, the headteacher's positive action plan was endorsed; subject to governor involvement on the equal opportunities working party and quarterly reports of its progress to the governing body.

## ■ Progress, what progress?

The headteacher was convinced from the outset that any progress would be slow and long-term since she acknowledged, with members of her staff and governing body, that the real problem lay in the wider society. However, she was adamant that the school could not abstain from its responsibility to society. During the first year of the equal opportunities working party's life the following positive action points were made:

1   Equal opportunities was the major agenda point at the annual meeting of parents. This led to an open discussion under the question 'What can we do – together?'

2   The school reviewed the ways in which it celebrated achievement; this led to a more public recognition of success at all levels of the school.

3   Staff development time was given to departments to produce differentiated teaching materials.

4   The ratio of support teacher lessons was increased in Key Stage 3.

5   Target-setting was introduced to teaching and tutoring in Y7 and Y8.

6   Non-stereotypical images of men, women and those from ethnic minority backgrounds were displayed around the school and in curriculum areas.

7   Local businesses were asked to complement this commitment to non-stereotypical behaviour at the careers fair.

8   A multi-cultural day was mounted in the summer term.

9   An 'assertiveness for women' course was made available for members of staff, sixth form and Y11.

10  The head of home economics was promoted, after internal interviews, to the post of head of technology.

BUT,

1   Males continued to underperform females at GCSE.

2   Fewer females completed science subjects at 'A' level.

3   No males enrolled on catering, caring or service courses post-16.

4   One more case of racial harassment was reported.

5   The post of head of science went to a male since no females with adequate experience applied.

# C9
# Managing progression and continuity in the National Curriculum

The terms 'progression and continuity' trip lightly off the tongue, but are rarely defined in such a way as to clarify the difference and the relationship between them.

At an Academic Board Meeting (the body which had previously been known as the heads of department meeting, see D5) in Abbeydown School, the head of mathematics was presenting the department's scheme of work for Key Stage 3 for comment and approval. She explained that, the more her department had considered it, the more they were convinced that progression and continuity lay at the heart of the National Curriculum. After all, students would in a few years come from primary schools with the 'luggage label' of National Curriculum levels of attainment, and parents would expect to see their child's learning programme differentiated from that of other students with different attainment. When pressed to define terms, she proposed:

- **continuity**: the logical sequencing of topics/content, especially but not exclusively at points of potential disjuncture (change of year, teacher or especially primary —> secondary) to ensure . . .

- **progression**: the individual's pathway through the scheme of work, ensuring that s/he has strengths built on and consolidated and weaknesses addressed, and is thus constantly developed and challenged at his/her own level.

The head of mathematics saw continuity as being more a teacher-based concept, concerning writing the scheme of work whereas progression was more at the individual student level.

In presenting the scheme of work, continuity therefore posed little problem, particularly in a structured subject such as mathematics, although the process of agreeing the scheme was laborious. She explained the sequence of decision-making in departmental meetings which had led to the topic order for Key Stage 3 proposed in her scheme:

1   We started with a blank sheet of paper – if we were setting about a revision of our scheme for Y7 – Y9, what changes would we want to make? In other words, let's try to make it as far as possible *our* change. Responses on paper to this question were called for from all department members before the first department meeting, together with a request to all to read the National Curriculum proposals carefully before that meeting.

2   A summary of responses was presented by the head of department at the department meeting, followed by discussion of Key Stage 3 programmes of study, attainment targets etc. This included points of clarification, did staff welcome the proposals, which areas seemed to be missing, which were new, how well did the proposed changes match with the changes the department wanted?

**3** A match of programmes of study against existing scheme of work and resources was undertaken by the second in department, and presented as draft to the next department meeting, together with proposals for changes and the identification of potential difficulties. With the modifications agreed at this meeting, this resulted in a draft set of topics for the three years.

**4** With the guidance of the headteacher, a small number of heads and Y6 teachers from partner primary schools were invited to discuss the proposal with the head of department and her number two. Primary colleagues suggested a number of ways in which the scheme could be streamlined by dovetailing better with their work. The discussion resulted in the setting up of a group involving staff from Abbeydown which would draw up Key Stage 2 schemes of work in mathematics across the partner school group.

**5** A late draft was then discussed by the head of department with the heads of science and geography, to see if further streamlining could take place, or if they had views on the order of content. Agreements were made concerning the timing of work on basic statistics by the maths department. It was also agreed that the geography department would undertake revision of work on graphs and coordinates.

**6** The department then met to do two things:

- finally to agree the topics to be covered in Y7–9;
- to put them into a logical sequence, and one which could be resourced – so that all staff would not require the same piece of equipment at the same time, but each could nonetheless manage the learning in an order which would make sense to students.

The final draft was then typed for presentation at the Academic Board Meeting. Following agreement, the plan would be used as the basis for ordering resources, and for bidding to the finance committee for a supplementary estimate if necessary.

The Academic Board Meeting agreed that this represented a model of good planning practice which other departments would attempt to emulate.

The head of mathematics then went on to outline how she and her department had approached the issue of progression through the Key Stage 3 programme. Since this is a matter of the individual's route through the work, they decided to manage it through the formative profiling process, linked to the record of achievement. They had planned four steps:

1   The collection of information about individual students' attainment as early as possible, through good liaison with primary partners. This would be detailed information, not just attainment level in Key Stage 2 SATs and entailed the drawing up of common proformae for the recording of attainments, strengths and weaknesses. These would then be talked through with the Y6 teacher, by the Y7 year head or form tutor. The proformae themselves would come into the mathematics department and be copied to all Y7 teachers, and individual cases discussed with the tutor/year head.

2   The design of the scheme of work in such a way that it promoted the use of varied teaching styles, differentiating for varied aptitude by process rather than merely graduating exercises, and thereby giving all students the opportunity to achieve.

3   Building in a review process – at intervals dictated by the work programme, not arbitrary dates in the school calendar, teachers of mathematics would sit with small groups of students in turn, and agree strengths to be consolidated, weaknesses to be addressed, and gaps to be plugged. The work programme would then be agreed.

4   Student and teacher would then update the record of achievement with a note of targets reached and new targets agreed. Since the record had been designed to be 'National Curriculum compatible', it facilitated writing reports to parents.

Lengthy discussion took place about the demands of such a process on teachers' time; concern was expressed about 'all paperwork, not enough teaching.' The head of mathematics was adamant that, although she was only too well aware of the burden, the National Curriculum only made sense if something along the lines the department proposed could be achieved. What was the point, she said, of bashing on with teaching the syllabus if there was no guarantee nor means of checking that progress was being made by the individual, and that s/he was having his/her real needs met?

She intended to make some time for her teachers by:

• the use of department meetings, including sub-teams, jointly to write materials. The Y7 teaching team could be freed one lesson per fortnight by a lead lesson being taught by one of their number;

• better use of INSET days; she intended to ask the Academic Board to recommend to the headteacher that at least half of the total time on the five days would be allocated to departments to address their particular needs;

• buying-in invigilators for examinations, freeing teachers to prepare;

- the coordination of *joint* updating of the scheme of work, and *joint* writing of materials and preparation of resource bids;

- as LMS spreads to departments, to discuss with other heads of departments the purchase of more non-teaching staff hours, as a cost-effective way of, for example, producing and maintaining stocks of teaching resources.

As well as agreeing the Key Stage 3 mathematics scheme of work, the members of the Academic Board agreed that this had been a useful way of spending a meeting and a vast improvement on old heads of department meetings. They had received some valuable INSET on curriculum planning, on numeracy and how they could support it through the work of their departments, and on departmental organisation.

It was agreed that the next meeting would be given over to a discussion of the Key Stage 3 science scheme of work, during which the heads of science and geography would explain how they had come to an agreement on the 'sub-contracting' of aspects of the science programmes of study to the geography department.

# C10
# Raising expectations: promoting quality across the school

This section is about basics, and about words which are more often used than analysed and addressed – like 'pace', 'rigour' and 'expectations'.

At a meeting of the senior management team of Abbeydown School, one of the deputies put the following item on the agenda:

*'Do we spend too much effort on caring for students, and not enough demanding high standards of them?'*

When asked to introduce the item, he explained that he was very anxious that the school should care for its students, but that part of caring for them – part of their entitlement – is to get the best from them. 'Increasingly,' he added, 'I worry that we don't challenge them academically. And I don't only mean the most able, I mean all students.' There was a good deal of head-nodding around the table, so the headteacher ran the item as a brainstorming session, to allow as many aspects as possible to be voiced. After all the various points were recorded, one colleague summed up accurately by saying: 'We seem to be saying three related things; first, that we've undertaken so much development work that we're concerned whether we've lost touch with the basics – brisk pace and rigorous demands in some of the basic operational features of the school; second, that although we're happy with the overall standards achieved in the school, we sense a certain complacency in the school, not necessarily among parents and governors – dangerous in the light of the rising reputations of other schools in the area; finally, we hear too often the siren voices which say 'you can't ask too much of kids round here'.

The follow-up action fell, understandably, to the deputy head who had raised the issue. The meeting deputed him to present a draft response to the next meeting. His paper follows:

---

### Raising expectations: promoting quality across the school

I started by planning an investigation into whether the three points we agreed on at the last meeting were true or not – whether we have lost touch with the basics etc – followed by a plan of action if we found we had. I came to the conclusion that investigating standards and trying to raise them had so much in common that it was probably better to assume that the three points were justified and get on with it!

My second conclusion was that there is an infinite number of aspects of the school we could focus on as evincing 'standards' or 'rigour', and that what we want is something manageable and punchy, involving all constituents, with a quick payback and the possiblity of continuing monitoring.

I therefore propose three approaches, each of which addresses one of our three concerns from the last senior management team meeting. I have proposed, as you will see in the schedule (Figure 8), that they are managed by what might appear to be slightly unlikely people. My purpose is to give as independent a view as possible, and not to be open to the charge of self- fulfilling prophecy, which might be the case if the senior management team managed them. The reports will be produced by the end of the first week in March, and I will top and tail them with explanation and plans for action. Although we may decide to vary the approach depending on what is in the reports, at this stage, I envisage issuing the report a week before the staff meeting at the end of March, to give five minutes at that meeting for each 'manager' to give a brief 'gloss' on her or his report, followed by a discussion of the proposed action and any continuing monitoring.

I have no doubt that staff will try to question the validity of the exercise or of the sample. We need to be very careful in data collection and presentation to be convincing.

| Area of investigation | Managed by timescale | Proposed methods | People involved |
|---|---|---|---|
| *Time on task* | LEA School adviser | Pupil pursuit – recording amount of curriculum downtime<br><br>Also to check on marking – amount and adherence to school policy | Probationers and student teachers also to follow students as part of their development programme, using a common schedule drawn up & briefed by adviser |
| *Homework* | Chair of PTA | Tutor check on % set in diaries in week beginning 18th Feb<br><br>Questionnaire to parents attending Y8 and 10 parents' evenings in Feb. on amount, type etc | tutors to year head for collation<br><br>PTA to administer on the evenings and collate results |
| *Academic demands on Y7 students* | Head of partner primary school | Sample of 9 students chosen from Y7, three from each broad ability band<br>Students to repeat tests taken in Y6<br>Heads/Y6 staff from their primary schools to take in their work for week beg. 18 Feb and compare it with work done in Y6 by those or current students and present their findings to investigation manager | head Y7<br><br>primary heads to administer<br><br>head Y7 to collect and deliver |

Figure 8

I suspect that, when the stone is lifted, some fairly nasty things will crawl out. The question arises as to what actions we can take to improve what is going on.

Part of the answer might lie with the continuing monitoring – collecting data on something often changes its behaviour.

We might find that we need to rewrite or enforce policies, such as on homework. We might find that students and staff are brisk about the building, but the 40 × 35 minute timetable just creates too many breaks in the day, losing us time. We need to keep an open mind, and not just rely on one strategy. Certainly we would be unwise merely to seem to criticise staff without praising too, and without apportioning 'blame' (although that is not the right word) elsewhere as well.

It would be more complex if the third investigation revealed that we set students back at transition, or have expectations of them which are too low. This would certainly have implications for our schemes of work, and for curricular and pastoral liaison with partner primary schools. It may be that we use this information, together with the replanning for the National Curriculum, consciously to raise our sights. Certainly, such a finding would create a major priority for the school development plan, and should be the subject of more detailed planning by a team including some who are not teaching staff here.

# C11
# Improving the performance of management

From the moment of her appointment, the headteacher of Abbeydown School was anxious to establish efficient and effective management in the school.

## ◼ Governance and management

She made it clear to the governing body that the first step should be to establish the precise boundary between governance and management. A number of governor sub-committees was established to complement the termly full governors' meeting. Thus, the following sub-committees met on a regular basis to service the full governors' meeting:

1    Finance sub-committee

2    Personnel sub-committee

3    Curriculum sub-committee

Later, a marketing sub-committee was created to coordinate the work of the school's marketing plan as it evolved (see Section C6).

A clear remit was established for each of these sub-committees to ease the work of the main meeting. The headteacher served on the finance sub-committee and delegated her two deputies onto the other two. Members of the governing body became involved on working parties concerned with matters of policy like equal opportunities (C8) and with curriculum review teams (B8 and C2). The governing body was as clear as the headteacher that it appointed her to manage and that its province lay in the making of the decisions that shape policy.

## ■ Management Structure

The senior management team of Abbeydown School, comprising the headteacher, two deputies and senior teacher, were given line management responsibilities for curriculum areas other than those in which they taught.

| | |
|---|---|
| Headteacher | Science, technology and learning support |
| Deputy head 1 | English, modern languages and mathematics |
| Deputy head 2 | Expressive arts and physical education |
| Senior teacher | Humanities and religious education |

These responsibilities were largely concerned with curriculum, resource and personnel review and necessitate regular contact with the departments in question in a formal and informal way. Contact with the departments was focused in two ways; through the monthly Academic Board Meetings and the weekly senior management team meetings.

The former were chaired by the three members of the senior management team, other than the headteacher, in rotation. As with all meetings in the school, full agendas were provided a week in advance of the meetings, minutes were taken by a member of the school's secretarial support staff and action points were apportioned to individual members of staff.

The weekly senior management team meetings were timetabled to last for a double lesson (an hour and a half) on a Thursday morning. The chairing of this meeting is the responsibility of deputy head 2 who was recognised as having the best chairing skills in the senior management team.

The agenda was, typically, concerned with five main points:

1   Governors' business

2   Curriculum matters

3   Causes for concern:
   • students
   • staff
   • community

4   Diary

5   Educational issues

There was no item entitled 'any other business'. Each agenda item was given in fuller detail in advance of the meeting with specific members of the team allocated to particular points. The fifth agenda item was led by a member of the senior management team in rotation and was concerned with an area of briefing, innovation or concern; this item was timetabled for the last 20 minutes of the meeting.

A full staff meeting took place on a monthly basis for an hour at a time. This meeting was concerned with matters of policy which relate to the school as a whole. Diary matters and causes for concern were dealt with at morning briefings or via the work of the heads of department. The full staff meetings were led by members of the senior management team in rotation and they made use of a variety of approaches to encourage active participation by the staff as whole.

All members of staff have specific job descriptions based upon the school's generic job description for classroom teachers; this is also true for the headteacher. These documents are a starting point for the school's staff development interviews and staff appraisal system (see Section C13). Heads of department are expected to maintain regular contact with each member of their department as well as following the fortnightly cycle of departmental meetings – the minutes for which are forwarded to the relevant line manager on the senior management team.

## ▉ Management structure and management style

The headteacher of Abbeydown School is well aware that the success of a carefully constructed management structure depends upon the quality of management style. She is, therefore, committed to the development of the management potential of all of her staff and is careful to monitor how effective her management style is perceived to be by those who are managed.

All teachers receive a staff development interview as part of the appraisal cycle (see Section C13). These interviews seek to determine each individual's development needs in managerial terms. Such needs may be realised through wider responsibility, improved management approaches or particular training. In any event, a programme for development is the entitlement of each teacher. Some of these programmes are expensive, others relatively cheap; the headteacher believes that all are cost effective in terms of improved performance.

Each year, the senior management team's working practices are reviewed through a staff perception exercise which involves the use of questionnaires such as Heller's instrument in *Helping Schools Change* (Centre for the Study of Comprehensive Schools 1985). The team employs an external consultant on an annual basis to help it review staff perceptions, internal relationships, working practices and priorities. This review is usually focused at a residential weekend during the summer term.Those who have middle management responsibility are helped in their management development by their line managers. In addition, each will have the opportunity to partake in a management development course at some point. At best, the school seeks to place groups of three middle managers on such a course each year.

All teachers are regarded as managers – both real and potential. A support programme under the title 'self-management' is available through staff development time and through external providers. Aspects of 'self management' are provided each year for probationary and new teachers as part of their induction by the member of staff who has specific responsibility, under the staff development tutor (senior teacher), for new staff.

In addition, occasional courses are provided on aspects of whole school management in response to needs identified through the school development plan. Thus, the course 'assertiveness for women' was made available in response to the work of the equal opportunities working party (C8).

# ■ Management efficiency

The headteacher of Abbeydown School believes that individuals within the school should be given the opportunity to manage themselves and develop skills, competence and confidence as a result. The structure that has been put in place has been established to support individuals in the exercise of their autonomy. This view is as much concerned with the experience of students as with that of staff.

Each year, as part of the review of the School Development Plan, members of the governors' personnel sub-committee undertake a management efficiency audit. This exercise seeks to quantify the amount of time and resource allocated to management in the course of a year and to consider the effectiveness of this allocation. Thus, a survey takes place which gathers staff perceptions of the usefulness of the meetings and development opportunities that have been made available to them. Consequently, a raw cost figure can be placed upon 'management time' and a perception equated which considers 'time profitably spent', 'time wasted' and neither. During one year, staff evaluated management time in the following ways:

|  | Profitable | Wasted |
| --- | --- | --- |
| Senior management team weekend | 63% | 22% |
| Departmental review | 73% | 17% |
| Heads of dept meetings | 45% | 26% |
| Full staff meetings | 22% | 54% |
| Staff development interviews | 83% | 10% |
| Management development | 71% | 12% |
| 'Assertiveness for women' | 93% | 2% |

As a result of this data and the evaluations of INSET, the senior management team have been able to improve the cost effectiveness of their management style and ensure that colleagues are given time to develop their managerial autonomy.

# C12
# Reviewing the pastoral system

Departments are subject to regular review in all secondary schools, if only through the annual scrutiny of their examination results. In many schools, there is considerable investment in a pastoral system which is not subject to the same review. This section suggests some approaches which  may be applied, modified appropriately, to a vertical house system. A horizontal system was chosen because it is the more common

| Investigation | By Whom and How |
|---|---|
| **1  Definitions**<br>*What/who in your school is the pastoral system?*<br>*Year heads/assistants, tutors, one deputy head, careers, SEN?*<br><br>*What % of budget of: staffing, non-contact time; accommodation; ancillary support; incentive allowances; is spent on the pastoral system?* | when the development plan indicates that the pastoral system is for review, the senior management team, through its member i/c the pastoral system, could set this information out as part of the introductory paperwork.<br>Bursar will supply financial info. |
| The key questions then become:<br><br>*Is it what we planned?*<br>*Does it represent good value?*<br>*How will we know?*<br>*Who will manage the investigation?*<br>(Perhaps a small team including a year head, a couple of tutors, one a head of department and the other a standard scale teacher.) | |
| **2  Intentions**<br>*What is the pastoral system for? Its basic purpose is not as clear as that of the Maths Dept., but do we know and agree its general aims? Is it for:* | an investigation into the purposes of the system and the roles as perceived by staff, students, governors, parents, as well as by the senior mangement team, would be revealing. |
| • *students in difficulty*<br>• *the learning of all students*<br>• *the personal development of all students*<br>• *filtering discipline problems*<br>• *organising social education*<br>• *delivering a tutorial programme*<br>  *or what?* | *by interview and/or questionnaire, by the managing team.* |

The questioning then splits into three:
*Is it actually doing what we want it to do?*
*How well is it doing it, and what are the effects on the students?*
*Is it organised, managed and resourced to carry out this (these) function(s)?*

| **3  Reality**<br>*How do pastoral heads and tutors actually spend their time?* | sample to complete a diary together with comments |
| *How do the results compare with the intentions?* | |
| *How does the rhetoric of the role of the tutor stand up to scrutiny?* | the school often says that the pastoral tutor is the key person in the school for student and parent; design a number of 'acid tests' to see if this is borne out in reality, such as: |

Does the tutor normally do the following:
- alert parents to problems being met by their children, write and sign such letters, and see parents under such circumstances
- act as the first port of call at parents' evenings
- coordinate the profiling process and complete the record of achievement with the student
- stay with the tutor group for 5 (or even 7) years?

Are the intentions matched by resources? Does s/he have the time and the training to carry out the role?

This will surely emerge in the diary and questionnaire/interview above.

Does a rhetoric/reality gap emerge? If so, how best to resolve it? Modify intentions, redesign roles, train?

## 4 Quality
To ascertain how well the roles are being carried out is partly a matter of perception and partly of looking at the outcomes for the students.

Perception of what by whom?

a matrix of key people: students; parents; staff; governors; partner schools/colleges; other agencies with whom the system works (police, social services, EWO, educational psychological service, health services etc).

against key questions, phrased in an open and positive form, such as: 'this service (with its aims etc defined) is useful to us because it . . .; it would be even more useful if it . . .'

What outcomes which lie within the ambit of the pastoral system do we expect for students?

the review of a year group will cast some light on both the pastoral and the departmental system, as the account on page 104 shows.

## 5 Resourcing
Only when the school has looked at what it wants its pastoral system to do and how well it is doing it, is it possible to ascertain whether the system is properly resourced to carry out its functions.

Figure 9    Investigating the pastoral system

form of organisation. It also seems to us easier to build curricular links in a horizontal system. Many schools now see their former heads of upper and lower school as coordinators of the key stages of the National Curriculum, with a role which spans oversight of the coherence of the curriculum for their students, as well as of their social and academic welfare and progress.

This section concerns the review of the working of the staff in the pastoral system (using Abbeydown School as an example), and of groups of students within it. We propose that a full investigation has the five parts shown in figure 9.

During discussions of priorities for the following year, the staff of Abbeydown School expressed a number of concerns over the first year (Y7). Some staff felt that the most able were not being identified or stretched, others that clear and firm standards of dress, behaviour and work habits were not being set, others again that the enthusiasm and abilities of the students were not being picked up and built on. The head was unwilling to make piecemeal changes to timetable or systems on the basis of opinion alone, much of it anecdotal and some contradictory. In order to make changes on the basis of evidence, to involve staff in research and decision-making, and to further links with primary partners at the same time, she invited the 'standing conference' of primary heads in the area to nominate one of their number and a teacher of a Y6 class in a different school, to join with a team consisting of the head of Y11 (to be head of Y7 next year), a current Y7 tutor and the head of science (a non-tutor this year) to investigate and make recommendations. The team met after school on a couple of occasions, discussed carefully with colleagues both in Abbeydown and the primaries, and came up with a strategy. They decided:

1    There were two main concerns:

- that the achievements of the children leaving school were not picked up quickly, leading to 'marking time' for some, loss of motivation and a slip in standards for others;

- that not enough was being demanded of first year students, in terms of work, behaviour, responsibility etc.

2    There would be two main investigations, one of the present Y7, the other of the transfer procedure at next summer. For the latter, the focus would be the quality, uniformity across the 'pyramid' and use made of the information passed at transfer. For the former, a 'focus week' was chosen, without the knowledge of anyone outside the investigating team. During the week, the following studies will be carried out:

- % of the year group receiving whatever rewards and sanctions the school operates;

- % of year group participating in extended curricular activities;

- a sample of students of all abilities and attainments to bring all its work for the week to the team on the Monday of the following week; they will work out the % of homework set and marked, and the Y6 teacher of each student will be asked to comment on the standards of work – content, quality and presentation – in the light of her/his records;

- staff from both the primary and the secondary sector, and students, will be asked to comment on their views of Y7 work.

3   The reporting should be as anonymous as possible, and in the form of a brief set of main findings and recommendations for action, with their reasonable resource implications. The team will hopefully be invited to address staff meetings in each partner school on the report.

4   The process would be general rather than subject-specific, but it might well lead on to a programme of more specific investigations in future.

Getting working parties and study groups to strike a balance between reports which are no more than a plea for resources – 'if we had . . . then we could . . .' – and those which ignore all resource implications, is a matter of training. As staff become used to systematic self-evaluation and to the fact that the budget implications of one desirable development are in competition with those of another, and particularly when these demands on the budget are opened to the staff, so the quality of the response will improve.

# C13
# Linking staff development and appraisal to the school development plan

For many years, staff development at Abbeydown School had been haphazard. A member of the senior management team had been given responsibility for this aspect of personnel management. A corner of the staffroom noticeboard was dedicated to 'Courses and INSET'. Staff development days were organised by the senior management team and provided opportunities for departmental development as well as opportunities to address whole-school issues. In addition, an induction course was available for teachers new to the school during their first term which extended throughout the year for probationary teachers.

With the advent of the school development plan and the scheduled introduction of appraisal to Abbeydown, the headteacher decided that it was time to review current approaches to staff development. Her basic purpose was to tie practice into the cycle of review and improve the quality of support given to the professional growth of individual teachers.

## ■ Appraisal at Abbeydown School

The majority of staff were keen to implement an approach to appraisal at the school as soon as possible. There was a feeling that, under the previous headteacher, little heed had been taken of individual needs and that 'management don't really know what concerns us at the chalkface'. One of the targets that the new head set herself on appointment was to establish staff appraisal within her first three years in post. In order to take staff with her, she placed a clear plan for implementation before them which itemised the way forward to a fully functioning system by the end of her third year in post.

The following approach was adopted –

| | |
|---|---|
| Initial staff meeting to raise issues | October 1989 |
| Staff development day | |
| – Appraisal Awareness – | November 1989 |
| Identification of pilot appraisers | February 1990 |
| Pilot appraiser training | March to June 1990 |
| Pilot appraisal – first stage | October to December 1990 |
| Pilot appraisal interviews | February to March 1991 |
| Pilot report to governors and staff | May 1991 |
| Full headteacher appraisal | May to June 1991 |
| Further appraiser training | June 1991 |
| Full appraisal – first stage | October to December 1991 |
| Full appraisal interviews | January to March 1992 |
| Appraisal documentation to senior | |
| management team | April 1992 |

A full staff development day devoted to appraisal awareness made use of an appraisal trainer and witnesses from outside school to itemise the purposes, processes and pitfalls of appraisal. As a result, the school was able to agree upon an appropriate pilot system with the governing body.

Pilot appraisal took place in four volunteer departments that were eager to experiment with approaches. They followed all the procedures that might have become a part of the fully-fledged system, but there was an agreement that any paperwork would be shredded at the end of the pilot process. Deputy headteacher 2 took responsibility for the management and evaluation of this pilot.

The pilot procedures involved all of the following stages –

1   Initial meeting

2   Self-review

3   Information gathering

4   Lesson or task observation

5   Appraisal interview

6   Agreed statement and targets

Since the headteacher was keen to take a lead, she suggested that she would wish to be involved in her own appraisal with a peer headteacher and a member of the LEA at the later stages of the school's pilot.

After the pilot appraisal period, a number of changes were made before full implementation; these included the following requirements:

- further training in classroom observation and feedback;

- improvements in self-review prompts and final documentation;

- greater security for agreed statements and targets;

- the need to link staff development to appraisal.

## ■ Linking staff development to appraisal

Once full documentation was available to the senior management team in April 1992, it was possible to match department and individual staff needs to the School Development Plan. The cycle of internal review had led to the publication of the annual School Development Plan in March. A statement of each department's development needs appeared in each of their development plans.

It was the responsibility of deputy headteacher 2 to draw up the Staff Development Plan over the Easter holiday. He gathered together the individual and departmental needs and identified strands which were appropriate to the school as a whole. These he allocated to possible staff development days or directed meeting time.

The needs of departments were dealt with equitably, with particular requirements receiving favourable time and resource allocation. For example, training in National Curriculum assessment was, in that year, a priority for the mathematics and science departments. In most cases, departments had scanned the LEA and other providers' INSET handbooks to locate relevant courses; the deputy headteacher did a further scan to identify courses that appeared 'interesting'.

Development courses which pertained to individual staff needs were considered. In some cases, such courses were available for teachers, like the LEA support programme for probationary teachers. In other cases, the school sought to buy in specific courses in conjunction with neighbourhood schools, for example, a development course for middle managers provided by external consultants. Finally, the school sought to make use of in-house training, for example by providing supply cover to enable a group of teachers on the Equal Opportunities Working Party to follow students for a day.

The deputy headteacher with responsibility for staff development was able to publish his draft programme for the year from April 1992 to the school's heads of department immediately after Easter. With a few amendments, this was published to staff in the second week of the summer term.

A full staff meeting took, as its main agenda item, the school's policy for staff development. At this meeting, the commitment to professional management development for all staff was restated. All members of the teaching and non-teaching staff were asked to express their satisfaction or otherwise with their individual programmes during the upcoming appraisal cycle.

# C14
# Responding to the Parent's Charter

When the Parent's Charter first arrived at Abbeydown in the autumn of 1991, it aroused a degree of cynicism in the staff. Was this not a party

manifesto? Did it not make the presumption that schools had deliberately kept parents in the dark, or at least on the far side of the school
gate? Where was the concentration on parental responsibilities as well as
parental rights?

However, a number of strands within the school development planning process over the previous three years had hinted that parental partnership was not all it might be. The study of transition from primary
schools had revealed some serious parental misapprehensions about life
at Abbeydown. There persisted a number of parental concerns which the
Abbeydown staff thought had died years before. An investigation into
homework brought forth some criticisms from parents, and the study of
turn-out at parents' evenings revealed a serious fall-off in attendance by
parents of students higher up the age range and lower down the ability
range.

The headteacher decided to tackle the issue of parental support and
involvement head on, and so raised it at all the meetings in one cycle –
the PTA, the governors, and the staff. The Charter came up in discussion
at all of these meetings. Despite still having reservations about it as a
document, the headteacher proposed using the Parent's Charter as both
a checklist for the school's offering to parents and a focus for the discussion of partnership with parents.

A seminar was therefore arranged by the head, involving representatives of all the school's main constituents, to ask the question: 'What is
the meaning and importance of the Charter for our school?' They came
to the conclusion that it attempted to define one side of a contract – the
rights of the parental half of a partnership with the school to enhance the
education of students. Their proposal for action was twofold:

1   To invite an honest appraisal of the school's performance against
    the terms of the Charter, and to act on the findings.

2   To write the other half of the partnership or contract – the
    parental response.

The group had it in mind to register both of these ideas in the school
prospectus – by seeking the 'Chartermark' for the school, as soon as
details became clear, and by spelling out the terms of the contract with
parents. The school would guarantee certain levels of parental information and involvement, while the parents would guarantee to support
their children at school in a number of ways. Without being so pompous
as to say so, the school was drawing up a 'charter' of its own. The first
draft of the contract, produced by a working group of parents, students,
governors and teachers and offered widely by them for consultation,
read as follows:

## ABBEYDOWN SCHOOL: PARTNERSHIP BETWEEN SCHOOL & PARENTS

Abbeydown School believes that students achieve their best when school and family work together, and that parents have the right to know what is going on in their school and for their children. The staff, students, parents and governors of the school have devised this **ten-point plan to involve and inform parents**

All parents will receive:

1   a detailed annual written report on their child's progress and perfor-mance in each subject s/he studies, including specific comments on work attitude and contribution to school life;

2   an annual opportunity to study their child's profile – the record of her/his progress against targets agreed with the teachers, compiled by the student her/himself and commented on by teachers;

3   In years 7 and 8, an annual opportunity to meet their child's tutor to dis-cuss his/her progress; from year 9 upwards, this parents' meeting includes all the subject teachers as well as the tutor;

4   Parents who are concerned for any reason about their child's progress or welfare need not wait for these annual meetings, but may come in at any time to meet with their child's tutor or year head. An appointment makes life much easier for us all, but if you are worried, just come in and talk with us;

5   an annual written report from the governors on the progress of the school as a whole. This will include:

   • a detailed account of the school's performance in national tests and exams at 14, 16, 17, and 18, its attendance rate, and the destinations of its leavers. These figures will be compared with those for all other schools in the area;

   • an outline of the school's priorities for the previous year, how they were tackled, and the priorities for next year;

   • in the year of the school's inspection (see 7), the governors' report will also include a summary of the inspectors' report, and a copy of the school action plan – what we propose to do in response to what the inspectors have said;

6   an opportunity to meet with the governors to discuss their report.

7   a summary of the school's four-yearly inspection report, and access to the full text, together with an opportunity to meet with the leader of the

inspection team before the inspection to raise concerns which her/his team may follow up during the inspection;

**8**   regular structured opportunities to give your views on the school, its policies and its future development (see B9);

**9**   an annual brochure about the school, listing staff and governors, and giving details of the school's approach to everything from uniform to sex education;

**10**   the opportunity to join the Friends of Abbeydown – an association of parents, teachers and friends of the school, whose aim is to help the school to develop. The association supports parents as well as running social events, raising funds for the school and keeping parents informed on developments in education. We do hope you will all join.

This is not an exhaustive list of what's available – there are plays, concerts, exhibitions, newsletters . . . but the ten points are the main ways we keep communication open between us. By fulfilling these ten points, we more than meet the terms of the Parent's Charter, copies of which you received in 1991. We shall be applying for the Chartermark to go on our prospectus, showing that we meet the highest standards of service.

In return, we ask that parents

- ensure that their child attends school regularly, and keep the school informed when s/he cannot;
- attend as many of the events above as they can;
- take an interest in the work of their child and the activities of the school;
- create the best conditions possible for homework – we do understand that a quiet room with a desk is just not possible for all, and ask that you let us know if conditions are difficult. We may be able to organise for him/her to do homework at school;
- check and return the homework diary on a weekly basis, making any comments you wish;
- help us keep to the school dress policy;
- come and complain to us first, and give us a chance to explain and/or put it right.

# Instruments

## D1
## Observing teaching

### ▇ Introduction

The success of schools rests entirely upon the provision of quality teaching and learning. While schools, and external agencies, have become adept at analysing performance data, such as examination results, little has been done to evaluate the effectiveness of classroom practice. However, some schools have begun to encourage teachers to observe lessons and to gather information about the learning experience as seen from the student's point of view.

Teachers are freed from their teaching commitments for a day in order to follow a particular student; to experience the day from the student's point of view and gather hard data to inform further developments in respect of the management of teaching and learning.

In most schools, teachers are unused to other adults in their classrooms. Consequently, it is essential that the reasons for, and practice of, such an approach are dealt with sensitively and positively by the management of the school. A direct lead should be taken by a member of the senior management team of the school to explain the reasons for such activity to the whole staff and to make it clear what the exercise is aiming to do and, moreover, what it is *not* aiming to do. Thus, an explanation which stresses the need to see the school from the students' point of view as a way of developing greater professional effectiveness begins to convince those staff who fear that 'someone is checking up on us'.

Caution, uncertainty and awkwardness are apparent when the idea of classroom observation is raised in schools where teachers are unused to sharing their teaching with other colleagues. Concerns arise when teachers fear that they are being measured, assessed or appraised. Any defensiveness can negate the whole exercise; teachers may behave unnaturally in the classroom, use material which is uncharacteristic of their usual teaching and even second guess the preferences of the observer. It is important that such tendencies are limited. Nevertheless, the arrival of an 'outsider' does contaminate the naturalness of the classroom atmosphere *for a while*. In the experience of the authors, students and teachers soon forget the presence of an 'outsider' once the teacher allows himself/herself to perform 'as normal'.

In the more cautious schools, probationary or inexperienced teachers are often equipped as the first teachers to conduct pupil pursuits, in order to minimise the sense of 'threat'. It is clear that the more often professional and supportive observation takes place, the more natural the experience is for both teachers and students. In schools where such a practice is much used, it is common to hear teachers say – 'We've always got people in our lessons; it makes no difference to us at all.'

## ■ Gathering hard data

The most important principle of classroom observation is that the observer is not seeking to make judgements but rather to gather hard data about what he/she observed *from the student's point of view*. It is for the teacher who has been observed to draw conclusions and judgements about the student's experience on the basis of the data presented.

It is essential that the observer has a prepared observation schedule in order to focus the experience of a student's learning. It is all-too-easy for key elements in a student's experience to pass unnoticed if the observer enters the classroom with the objective of making random notes. Observed teachers find hard data more useful for their future development than any amount of subjective generalities. Under some circumstances, it may be desirable for these to be a single agreed focus for the observation. For example, a teacher may be interested in the effectiveness of group-work which she/he is unable to observe objectively whilst teaching a lesson. In these cases, the teacher might plan the nature of the observation schedule with the colleague who is to perform the observation. Such a practice is highly desirable and can lead to excellent professional development through **action research** (see Section D6). Under most circumstances, the focus will be wide-ranging; leading to a more exact enquiry as the school and the individual teachers become comfortable with the use of student pursuits to aid professional development.

The observation schedule provided below (Figure 10) has proved to be a useful way of gathering data from classroom observation. Essentially, a single piece of A4 paper for each lesson offers an aide memoire and sufficient space to record a significant amount of data, as can be seen from the sample completed sheet. The plan of the seating arrangement in the classroom allows the observer to record the position of males and females and to log responses by individuals to the teacher's questions, when classroom discussion takes place. The 'whirlpools' around

*PUPIL PURSUIT    DATE*:                *LESSON*:            *CLASS*:            *PUPIL*:

*Environment*:

*Resources*:

*Questioning*:

| Open | Closed | Functional |
|------|--------|------------|
|      |        |            |

Responses ♂                    ♀

X = ♀            y = ♂            T = teacher

| Mins | Teacher led | Individual | Group | NoA |
|------|-------------|------------|-------|-----|
| 1–3 |  |  |  |  |
| 4–6 |  |  |  |  |
| 7–9 |  |  |  |  |
| 10–12 |  |  |  |  |
| 13–15 |  |  |  |  |
| 16–18 |  |  |  |  |
| 19–21 |  |  |  |  |
| 22–24 |  |  |  |  |
| 25–27 |  |  |  |  |
| 28–30 |  |  |  |  |
| 31–33 |  |  |  |  |
| 34–36 |  |  |  |  |
| 37–39 |  |  |  |  |
| 40–42 |  |  |  |  |
| 43–45 |  |  |  |  |
| 46–48 |  |  |  |  |
| 49–51 |  |  |  |  |
| 52–54 |  |  |  |  |
| 55–57 |  |  |  |  |
| 58–60 |  |  |  |  |

*Reading*:

*Writing*:

*Talking*:

*Doing/Making*:

*Nature of Group-work*:

Figure 10    Proforma for observing teaching

*PUPIL PURSUIT*   *DATE*: 20.1.91   *LESSON*: 3   *CLASS*: $7_z$   *PUPIL*: John Adams

X = 13 ♀      y = 15 ♂      T = teacher

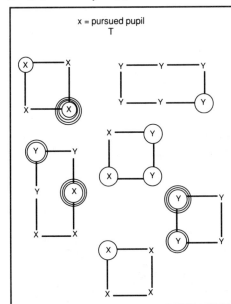

*Environment:*

Display: <u>Commercial</u> – Poster picture
                Technical
                diagrams
        <u>Pupil work</u> – dilapidated and
                aged, not marked

*Resources*: <u>Books</u> – Some fiction and
            topic/project books

<u>Resources for learning</u> – Well sorted,
w'sheets and cards coded for pupil access
<u>Reference material</u> – Topic books from
Lib. dictionaries, Thesaurus, Atlases
<u>Audio-visual</u> – 3 audio tape recorders -
headphones, tape bank, ohp, slide
projectors
<u>Computers</u> – 2 BBCs on movbable
trolleys, software keyed to lesson – used
by 5 pupils in lesson.

*Questioning:*

| Open | Closed | Functional |
|------|--------|------------|
| II | ~~HHT~~ ~~HHT~~ <br> ~~HHT~~ | III |

Responses 10 ♂        10 ♀

| Mins | Teacher led | Individual | Group | NoA |
|------|-------------|------------|-------|-----|
| 1–3 | | | | ✔ |
| 4–6 | ✔ | | | |
| 7–9 | ✔ | | | |
| 10–12 | ✔ | | | |
| 13–15 | ✔ | | | |
| 16–18 | | ✔ | | |
| 19–21 | | ✔ | | |
| 22–24 | | | ✔ | |
| 25–27 | | | ✔ | |
| 28–30 | | | | ✔ |
| 31–33 | ✔ | | | |
| 34–36 | ✔ | | | |
| 37–39 | ✔ | | | |
| 40–42 | ✔ | | | |
| 43–45 | ✔ | | | |
| 46–48 | ✔ | | | |
| 49–51 | | | ✔ | |
| 52–54 | | | ✔ | |
| 55–57 | | | ✔ | |
| 58–60 | ✔ | | | |

*Reading*: from b'board 7–9: Instructions for
week's work and summary of information
from last lesson.
Collaborative reading from worksheets
21–27.
Following teachers reading from book to
class 36–45.
(pupil distracted off text for 3 mins the 9).

*Writing*: Copying 15–21 from b'board.
Making notes on behalf of group following
teacher reading 48–54. Notes haphazard
and unstructured – no sense of developed
note-taking skills.

*Talking*: 3 answers to teacher questions (all
closed).
As group member – paired for reading
                (21–27)
         – scribe for group of 6 following
           teacher's reading.
           offering little orally and copying
           points from discussion (2 of the
           6 involved).

*Nature of Group-work*: Collaborative,
Functional problem-Solving.

Figure 10a    Completed Proforma for observing teaching

individual positions will indicate the spread and concentration of responses. In addition, the grid labelled **Open / Closed / Functional**, allows the observer to record the nature of questions asked by the teacher; and beneath it to tally responses by males and females. The three-fold distinction in the nature of questions may be explained as follows:

- **Open** questions are those which invite a wide range of response. They encourage the expression of opinions and the generation of hypotheses within a potentially problem-solving framework.

- **Closed** questions are those which are concerned with the recall of information and the confirmation of knowledge. These questions tend to be the ones most often used by teachers, since much class-room discussion is generated from recap and the focusing of the pupils' experience.

- **Functional** questions are those concerned with classroom man-agement, such as 'Has everybody done their homework?'

The observer's ability to gather data such as this depends upon adequate training and experience.

The classroom plan affords sufficient space for further information to be logged, such as the movement of the teacher around the room and which students have contact with the teacher.

Beneath the classroom plan lies a grid which enables the observer to log the broad distribution of time during the lesson. Every three minutes, the observer ticks a line to indicate the nature of the learning experience during that period of time. Each column – Teacher-led / Individual / Group-work / No organised activity – is then added up to reveal the dis-tribution of experiences through the lesson. At the end of a day spent in pursuit of a student, the figures for each lesson are totalled to arrive at a profile of the day as a whole.

Space is available on the observation schedule to note aspects of the learning environment and resources. Further space is available to note details concerning the student's experience of language. Samples of the reading and writing that takes place can be gathered throughout the day and may provide useful data about the time spent reading and writing, the overall level and nature of such experiences and the development of basic and higher-order skills. Observations concerning the nature of group-work may shed light upon the individual teacher's management of students working in this way.

The data is of use initially for the individual observed teacher; it has further use, as exemplified in Section B1, as a stage in the drawing together of whole-school policies.

# ▮ The observer's role and responsibilities:

As has been stated, the teacher as observer needs to conduct him/herself with sensitivity and care if this approach to internal evaluation and professional development is to flourish and not be rapidly discredited. It cannot be stressed too often that the observer is merely recording what appears to be taking place, and not making qualitative judgements. It is essential that this is clear in the minds of all observers and those to be observed before the school embarks on student pursuits.

It is recommended that the observer speaks with the student who is to be pursued before the day begins. In this way, the student and his/her peers will more readily accommodate the 'stranger'. In addition, this helps the observer gain a fuller sense of the student's weekly timetable and ability. The student must be made to realise that he/she is not being 'checked up on' but that the observer is merely interested in seeing a day from a student's point of view.

The observer should also take the opportunity of talking with the teacher before the start of the lesson which is to be observed. If this cannot happen then the observer should speak to the teacher at the start of the lesson to ease the atmosphere and establish the basic ground-rules.

The ground-rules are that the observer:

- has established contact with the student in question and no further action needs to take place;

- will be seated in a discrete place within the classroom which will enable him/her to observe events without intruding upon the lesson, from either the student's or the teacher's point of view;

- may take the opportunity at a suitable moment to look at the student's past and present work;

- will make notes on the agreed proforma which can be shared with the teacher after the lesson.

At the end of the lesson, the observer should thank the teacher and take the earliest opportunity to share notes and offer a debrief. This may take up to half an hour if the teacher wishes to discuss the findings in detail.

It is clear that there are a range of skills which need to be developed in those teachers who are to act as observers: observation skills, listening skills, reflection and counselling skills. To embark upon classroom observation without careful training of staff is a recipe for disaster. As a means to professional development for both observer and observed it is second to none; it is, therefore, worthy of scrupulous preparation. The staff development or curriculum tutor within the school should take responsibility for the training of observers. This might include the viewing of videos of classroom practice to aid observation, followed by role-play debriefing sessions in which the appropriate listening and counselling skills are scrutinised and developed.

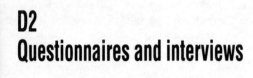

# D2
# Questionnaires and interviews

## Introduction

Much internal evaluation of school effectiveness relies upon subjective judgements gathered in a haphazard way. Consequently, the feelings of a few staff or the comments of a sample of students can be taken as representative of the true condition of a school. On the other hand, some schools will only measure their performance in terms of results and other statistical data. Clearly, there is room for the middle road. The opinions and perceptions of those involved in the life of a school – students, teachers, governors and parents – are valuable pointers to a school's effectiveness. These views are of value when questions are asked with care and represent a fair sample of opinion. The use of questionnaires and structured interviews provides valuable data to inform school improvement.

## Questionnaires

Of all evaluative tools, the questionnaire is most open to abuse or dismissal. If questions are not framed carefully or if the questionnaire is distributed insensitively, results will be contaminated and it will be impossible to use them reliably or to use such an instrument for future enquiries. Too often, questionnaires are seen as the easy way of gaining rapid information. In these circumstances, the design of the questionnaire is rushed, little attention is given to the kind of questions that need to be addressed and the resulting data is amorphous and difficult to process. As a result, those in receipt of the questionnaire often see it as a waste of their time and an invasion of their privacy.

The use of a questionnaire should be preceded by the following questions:

- What are we trying to find out?

- Why is a questionnaire the best way of gathering this information?

The successful answers to these questions should be concerned with the following desires:

- to sample the views of a large number of people;

- to gather data relatively quickly;

- to achieve a standardised, uncontaminated response;

- to offer anonymity of response;

- to draw a broad and generalised picture.

The design of the questionnaire should bear in mind the basic aims of the exercise as stated in the previous section. The questionnaire should make use of opportunities for closed and open responses. Closed responses are elicited by questions which require a YES/NO answer, or a DISAGREE/AGREE response, a tick-box answer, or reactions to a rating scale. Rating scales are best designed on a four-point scale since an odd number scale will tempt response to the middle. Thus, a question such as, 'Do you think that the school caters for individual students' needs?' might be asked with the request to respond on a four-point scale where 1 = *Rarely*, 2 = *Occasionally*, 3 = *Regularly*, 4 = *Always*. Where a series of rating scale questions are asked, it is advisable to use the same descriptors, or to ensure that the rating follows the same ascending scale from 1 to 4. Closed responses aid rapid interpretation but will only provide a broad, superficial picture. They provide the useful impetus for further, in-depth, enquiry.

Open response questions must be phrased carefully in order to elicit a response which is within the area of the enquiry. A question which is too open may lead to a response which does not relate to the enquiry, or to no response at all. Too much guidance or suggestion within the open question may produce a response which has been led by the framer of the questionnaire. In designing a questionnaire, one should be careful to avoid drawing the answers that one wishes to hear.

Clear instructions concerning how to fill in the questionnaire should be made at the outset. Thus, if a rating scale is used the recipient should be asked to circle the number which is nearest to her/his opinion. Those who are unused to rating scales should be asked to respond without too much thought and to rely upon their immediate reactions. Where an open response is required, adequate space should be given; sometimes aided by numbered point spaces to elicit a fuller but focused response. Some indication should be given of the length of time that the questionnaire is likely to take; under most circumstances, more than ten minutes is likely to be an excessive imposition.

Care should be taken over the language and appearance of the questionnaire. In the first instance, it is important that it is written in a style which is easily understood by the target audience. For example, a questionnaire eliciting a response from parents should not use language which is germane to educationalists. Equally, statements should be made which are unambiguous and lead to a clear response. The layout of questions and response spaces should be clear and attractive in order to invite an easy and confident approach by the recipient.

Reliable data is usually gained as a result of proffered anonymity. In other words, the recipient should not be required to divulge his/her name unless he/she wishes to do so. A statement at the close thanking the recipient for her/his time is a desirable act of courtesy.

As has been stated earlier, questionnaires can arouse suspicion and lead to defensive or dismissive responses. This may be diminished if the purpose of the exercise is made clear to the recipients so that they can be assured of its value and of the fact that they will be given feedback concerning the opinions and perceptions that have been gathered. It is important that such information is seen to be used for further evaluation and sensitive action.

# ■ Interviews

It may be that a sample of interviews is the consequence of a broad brush questionnaire survey of opinions. Interviews provide opportunities for more reflective and detailed responses. It is clear that fewer people can be targeted and that the views gathered can only be seen as a relatively small sample. It is important that care is taken in assembling the sample in order to ensure that the views expressed can be seen to be representative of a wider group.

The interview may be conducted in a variety of ways, ranging from the strictly structured to the informal. The tightly-structured interview ensures that the same questions are asked in the same way to all those who are interviewed. Such an approach may ensure consistency but may inhibit the free-flow of opinions. On the other hand, a totally informal interview may lead to a wide-ranging discussion which does not address the central issues. The most successful interview is one which covers a consistent regime of questions in a way which does not inhibit the natural flow of discussion. Such an interview demands considerable skill on the part of the interviewer. Such skill can only be acquired through careful preparation and practice. Once prepared, questions may be given to the interviewee in advance of the interview. This will lead to considered responses but may hamper the flow of spontaneous opinions and ideas. Equally, the interviewee may feel that much is expected of him/her and may resent the amount of time given to their preparation. Without prior sight of the questions, the interviewee may feel under-prepared and exposed. The best circumstances would be to give the questions in written form for half an hour before the discussion begins – always supposing that such time is available.

The time to be given to the interview should be made clear from the outset; the interviewer should keep to time and make sure that all of the required areas are covered. The setting for the interview should be attended to with care. Ideally it should be neutral space which will not be prone to interruptions (including the telephone) and which will allow for the use of positive body language. The interviewer should avoid using a desk as a barrier, should sit at the same level as the interviewee, should make use of eye contact and natural supportive language to encourage and refine responses.

An interview which lasts for anything up to half an hour will cover a lot of areas, many of which will be forgotten unless some means are used to record responses. Note-taking within a prepared proforma is often acceptable to the interviewee provided that courtesies have been established beforehand. The interviewer should avoid writing all the time since that will lead to inappropriate body language. Equally, long pauses while the interviewer scribes key points will hinder the flow of the interview. A simple checklist can be prepared so that responses can be recorded in a simple summary way without prejudicing the flow of the discussion. In some instances, the use of audio or video recording is acceptable, but this may be inhibiting and may over-complicate the servicing of the data since the time taken by the interview may be doubled or trebled.

There are occasions when the interview is best conducted with more than one person and takes on the flavour of a discussion led by the interviewer who, with skill, can take a back seat once the flow of discussion has been established. A discussion with a group of students will be less inhibiting to them than a one-to-one interview and will often lead to the sharing of unsolicited views. The interviewer should not feel, however, that such an interview requires limited preparation; the success of all interviews depends upon care before, and concentration during, the interview.

Above all, the interviewer should remember that he/she is seeking to gather information and should not, therefore, lead the discussion towards a prescribed outcome. The skill of the interviewer lies in the way s/he frames questions and encourages the interviewee to respond. It is always useful to keep the amount of time during which the interviewer is speaking in strict check. The most important attribute of a successful interviewer is the ability to listen actively, positively and sincerely. Listening skills should be practised and honed by any managers who wish to use evaluative skills to aid school improvement.

# D3
# Quality criteria

# Introduction

Evaluation of any aspect of school management or curriculum is best achieved in the context of clearly-stated criteria. Unfortunately, most external inspection and internal self-evaluation programmes rely upon subjective or covert criteria. This makes it difficult for schools to measure their efficiency and effectiveness in a developmental way. The business of assuring school improvement becomes chance and haphazard. Given a set of criteria for aspects of school organisation, a school has an objective means by which to evaluate itself.

Currently available criteria appear as checklists or questions; these are useful foci for evaluation but are rarely valuable tools for a school's development and improvement. Examples of 'quality criteria' for curriculum areas used by Californian Schools (*Quality Criteria for High Schools*) make use of such checklists organised as two-level criteria for 'effective' and 'ineffective' curriculum practice. The following example is from *Program Characteristics for Foreign Language Teaching*:

**Effective**: The language of the teacher and all learning materials are representative of what is heard and read in societies where the language predominates. Significant literature serves as the source of much of the language used and modelled and is chosen to enhance students' general knowledge and understanding.

**Ineffective**: The language used is contrived and out of context. It is chosen to illustrate certain linguistic forms and patterns. Literature is often translated and often chosen for its aesthetic reputation or grammatical structures.

Such an approach is useful but encourages a deficiency approach to evaluation; aspects of performance are categorised as good or bad and lines of development are not apparent.

# ■ Four-level positional statements

If two-level 'quality criteria' encourage a polarised approach to evaluation, criteria organised on three levels are little better. Given three points on a scale, the evaluator is tempted to choose the middle way. A more useful range is four-fold. Thus, when evaluating 'teacher-led learning' one might use the following four-level positional statements:

**Level 1**: The teacher is the focus of learning for the students. Instruction with little whole-class discussion is characteristic. Little attention is paid to encouraging effective or active listening by the students. The teacher rarely changes the tone of the delivery and frequently uses inappropriate vocabulary and syntax.

**Level 2**: More than a third of the lesson is spent on teacher-focused activity. Class discussion predominates, with the vast proportion of questions posed by the teacher being closed. Responses by students are usually confined to short answers confirming knowledge recall. Few questions are asked by students.

**Level 3**: Teacher-focused activity is an important part of the lesson. A clear statement of the lesson's objectives by the teacher at the outset is underpinned by focused discussion at critical points in the lesson. While closed questions are used, the teacher makes conscious use of open questions to encourage an enquiry-based, hypothesis-generating and problem-solving approach.

**Level 4**: Students' learning is managed in order to make best use of teacher-focused discussion which arises from individual or collaborative work. As a consequence, a high proportion of students of both sexes are actively engaged in teacher-focused talk in an enquiring environment. Students, as well as teachers, pose questions in an unthreatening and interested way.

Such a range of statements for the criterion 'teacher-led learning' could be organised within a quality criteria bank for 'effective teaching and learning' (see Section C1). Similar banks of criteria could be assembled on most aspects of school management and curriculum organisation. For example, quality criteria on four levels could be agreed for English, mathematics, science, design and technology, history, geography, religious education, foreign languages, art, music and physical education as well as for cross-curricular themes and dimensions. In addition, criteria for the school development plan, school communications and other aspects of management could be derived. Work developed by the Gloucestershire LEA Inspection Advisory Service exemplifies this model.

## ▓▓▓ Using four-level positional statements

The banks of four-level quality criteria for a curriculum area, a whole curriculum issue, or an aspect of school management can be used for rigorous and sharply focused self-evaluation.

Thus, the head of the science department within a school may agree upon a range of quality criteria that will be the focus of departmental review in a given year. One of the deputy headteachers within the school may assist the department with its self-evaluation on the basis of the agreed criteria. Following evaluation in the ways described under Section C2, the department should be in a position to conduct a review meeting (see Section B6) with members of the senior management team of the school. At the review meeting, the department head would be required to justify positions determined on the four-level scale for each of the agreed criteria. Having arrived at an agreed 'profile' for departmental performance, the department could be helped to prioritise for future development. Thus, from a criteria bank of (say) 20 they could choose their five priority areas. With senior management team guidance, they would be able to plan how they would propose to improve from one level to another in respect of the five priority areas. This would involve considerations of resources and staff development. Thus, the quality criteria would be the focusing instrument for development planning: evaluation, review, prioritising, target-setting and resource allocation.

The four-level positional statements should not be seen as providers of absolute truth. It may be that individual statements do not accord with the beliefs of individual teachers or departments. The statements should be viewed as foci for the dialogue which is an essential part of evaluation. Without such criteria there can only be a limited dialogue. With such criteria a range of opinions and approaches is available to help teachers define their attitudes and positions.

Clearly, it is a small step from using four-level quality criteria for evaluation to their use as a basis for policy writing. In this way, the quality criteria for 'effective teaching and learning' were used by Abbeydown School to derive a 'teaching and learning policy' (see Section C1).

# D4
# Sampling students' work

Monitoring the standards of work achieved by students should be a basic component of a school's quality assurance system. Nothing is more important than the quality of the product: student learning. The school will keep this under review in three ways:

1   Examination and test results (C3)
2   Classroom observation (D1)
3   Looking at work in progress

Whereas the first of these is an annual screening process, the other two involve sampling. This should be done on a rational basis, clearly understood by those taking part. It is likely that there will be a logical link between those students observed in class and those whose work is examined.

It is also worth noting at the outset that it is often extremely difficult to know whether you are looking at student or staff performance. The merit of looking at the whole work output of a student, and of looking at him/her in the classroom as well, is that inequalities in performance across the subjects are revealed, casting light on the degree to which what is being seen is the student's or the teacher's work.

Sampling students' work has the additional merit of raising senior staff interest and involvement at classroom level; the reduction of such involvement is a frequently voiced staffroom criticism of senior management. It also enables feedback to parents between regular report dates (*'As part of our weekly sampling of students' work, I have looked at Jane's current work, and I am pleased to be able to tell you that . . .'*), and helps keep staff and students on their toes.

A consistent message of this book has been that there is inherent merit in systems of evaluation which are **systematic**. Systems which are regular are designed to be manageable, and to become part of the bloodstream of the organisation. We would therefore suggest that whoever undertakes this role, sampling should be frequent and regular – a small number of students on a weekly basis may well be best.

There are two parts to the question 'who?' – which students, and which staff. There are four ways of choosing the student group:

- according to the priorities in the school development plan, for example, how do we challenge the most able? How high are our expectations for the least able? How demanding is the work for Y7? Each of these suggests a target group of students;

- with a focus on underperformers at the time of the last report;

- cyclically attempting coverage of all year and ability groups over a term or year;

- at random – which has little to recommend it.

Whose job is it within the school? There is no single answer, and yours may be determined by the reason for choosing the student group. A school development plan priority will have a managing group, and they might undertake the work sampling. Underperforming student follow-up will probably fall to the pastoral head or tutor. A whole year group focus might profitably be shared by the year head and the head of special educational needs or learning support, as part of her/his screening function. Cyclic coverage of the school may fall to year heads and/or the senior management team, or it may be the logical extension of the job description of the head of department that s/he samples the work of the students in the department on a regular basis. Linking both the observation of teaching and the sampling of students' work to the appraisal process may be possible, thus killing two birds with one stone.

The plea for a systematic approach is not a recipe for sterility. The school should certainly look to introduce variety into its system. The head or Y6 teacher from a partner primary school would give invaluable feedback on the work of students who used to be in that school (see also B8). Governors, post- 16 colleagues and others would make stimulating comments. A system cannot, however, be based on these occasional contributions, it must be managed by an individual or preferably a group inside the school.

The chosen group of students brings or sends all its workbooks and homework for the previous week to the appointed person, at the appointed time. Examples of art and design/technology and other practical work may be present, or the teacher may have to go to those areas of the school to carry out the necessary scrutiny.

How is sampling put into practice? Homework diary and profile sit on top of the pile of John Smith's books which confront you, the year head or deputy head with the job of assessing the quality of work. What are you looking for? What will you do?

Whatever the rationale for the process, two principles are vital:

- that the criteria should be published to all staff (and students);

- that some action is seen to result.

A suggested basic schedule for looking at the work follows. As in the rest of the manual, we have attempted to be realistic rather than exhaustive. It may well be that the reason for choosing this student group generates its own schedule; this list of questions assumes a cyclic look at general standards:

1   **Profile/report** What ability/motivation level is the student?

2   **Homework diary** Is it up-to-date, signed, complete? If 'none set' or blank, can this be corroborated or otherwise by reference to other students in the sample? Is the homework differentiated according to individual needs?

3   Follow up one or two listed homeworks in workbooks. Are they done? Marked? If so, to school policy?

4   How consistent is the care and presentation of work among subjects?

5   Although not easy to assess, can you get a feel for the volume of work being produced in the various subjects?

6   Is there a significant amount of incomplete work?

7   What impression do you get of the progress s/he is making? Based on whatever measures of attainment or ability you have, how is s/he performing?

8   Do trends seem to be appearing across subjects or across several students, such as homeworks which are predominantly the completion of classwork?

If the student accompanies his/her work, an invitation to show you work of which s/he is most proud normally initiates a most revealing dialogue about standards of work across the subjects. Care must be taken to keep the session courteous yet brief, and not to supplant or repeat the profiling process – unless of course these two processes are linked.

Without follow-up action, the process will be at best forgotten, at worst discredited, by staff. We do stress yet again that it must be kept to a small and manageable scale if it is to be maintained. Types of follow-up action include:

- a letter to parents;

- a note to tutor and/or profile or personal file of student;

- a regular brief report (oral or written) on general findings to staff;

- an annual detailed report on the sampling exercise;

- a contribution to self-evaluation documentation on a priority area;

- chase up staff or departments about standards or habits;

- a change to, or enforcement of, existing policies, eg homework;

- the writing of new policies, eg marking.

# D5
# Reading schemes of work and planning documents

Headteachers usually ask heads of department to provide the senior management team with a copy of their departmental scheme of work. Many of the subjects will not be the specialist area of the head or deputies, and so they will not be the best judge of the suitability of the content of the scheme.

The headteacher of Abbeydown School found on her arrival a box file labelled 'Departmental syllabuses'. In it was a mixture of examination syllabuses, detailed schemes of work and lists of content – of various dates, with some undated. The National Curriculum had already caused some departments to begin rewriting their schemes; others were poised to begin. The head was anxious to use the opportunity of this wholesale revision to develop schemes which would be more valuable to all users. When the senior management team met to discuss the issue, they began with three questions:

1   Why do we believe departments need these documents?

2   Why does the senior management team want a copy of them?

3   What should the senior management team be looking for when reading them?

They rapidly came to the conclusion that it would be good management to make their requirements for schemes of work clear in advance to those who would be responsible for writing or revising them. The following is the guide to writing schemes of work issued by the head of Abbeydown School.

## THE SCHEME OF WORK

All schemes of work should be stamped boldly 'DRAFT' or 'PROVISIONAL', to acknowledge the crucial importance of revision in the light of internal evaluation and external syllabus change.

### Question 1  Why produce a scheme of work?

There is often no clear connection between courses and individual lessons on the one hand, and school and department aims and objectives on the other.

An effective scheme of work will make this connection and will:

- act as a checklist for evaluation of the fulfilment and success of the programme;
- promote debate within the department about its work;
- clarify the contribution of the subject to the whole curriculum;
- promote a coherent education for the student.

In addition, the document will help in routine matters such as supporting new teachers, supply teachers, etc.

### Question 2  Who is it for?

Although the documents should be available to, and may be required by, the senior management team, the governors, and officers of the LEA, the prime purpose is to produce a *working, practical and supportive document for the teaching team*, not one which is glib, glossy or high-minded to sell or defend the department.

It is worth asking whether such documents should be available to students, parents, other departments, partner schools, local business etc., and if indeed any of these groups might have comments or contributions to make.

Accepting that the headteacher is ultimately responsible for seeing that such planning takes place, the task of writing falls inevitably and properly on the members of the teaching team. Although the head of department will take the lead and co-ordinate, there is every advantage in securing the full involvement of all team members. Such team work will facilitate:-

- pooling of resources and expertise;
- use and dissemination of individual expertise;
- effective use of limited time;
- staff development, through members of departments taking responsibility as course leaders for units or sections – drafting the scheme of work; collecting, assembling and making available resources; recommending changes, setting examinations, etc.

All team members can then comment on drafts produced by sub-groups, before a final version is produced. The head of department will share in this process, as well as ensuring that roles are defined and tasks set, that sub-groups adopt common practices and format, and that the work of sub-groups is compatible and produces a coherent whole.

### Question 3  What is a scheme of work?

The last section presupposes that, whereas the work of the department from year 7 to year 11 or 13 should be compiled into a full scheme of work, the task is sub-divisible into sections – a GCSE course, a self-contained package for Key Stage 3 – and further into units of a few weeks' duration. It is to these individual units that the remainder of this document gives its attention.

*'An inability to plan individual lessons effectively is one of the recurring weaknesses identified in published school reports . . . lesson planning can only be effective if syllabuses and schemes of work are used by the teacher to guide, structure and evaluate practice in the classroom. Within the carefully planned syllabus or individual lesson, the confident and competent teacher will also recognise the need for a spontaneous response . . .'*

*Education Observed* 3: para 19 HMSO, 1985

Presumably such a teacher will also recognise that the pace and strategy of delivery will have to vary in response to particular groups or individuals.

These thoughts guide our thinking on the nature of a scheme of work; it should facilitate the ability to 'guide, structure and evaluate', stressing targets and the means of achieving them, rather than stultifying the initiative of teachers and denying the individual needs of pupils by producing blow-by-blow lesson plans or blueprints.

A scheme of work should be set in a context of planning documents – the school development plan; school and department aims; broad learning objectives for the school or department; homework, record-keeping and marking policies.

### Question 4  What should be in a scheme of work?

Figures 11 and 12 which follow are checklists for the compilation of a scheme of work. The final section is an expansion of ideas from the

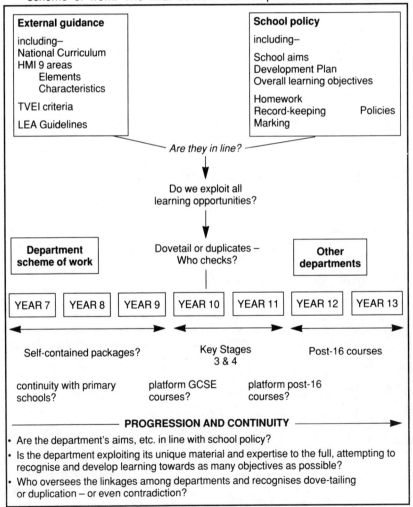

Figure 11    Checklist 1: *Context of a department scheme of work*

diagrams, together with a series of questions to be addressed by those compiling schemes of work.

The second diagram is a 'contents table' for a scheme of work. It suggests that there might be six headings under which each unit is described and analysed. Each of these headings is examined in a little more detail after the diagram.

It will be clear that, if a department's work is to be organised in this way, the kind of team approach described under Question 3 is essential.

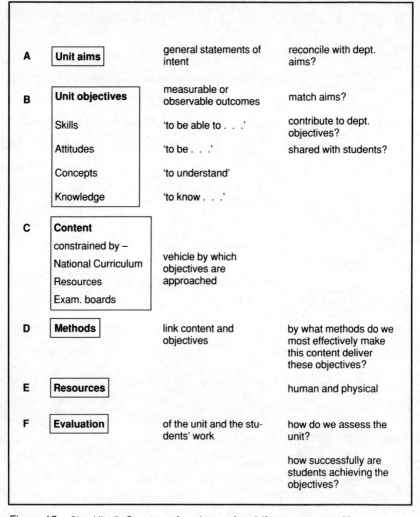

Figure 12    Checklist 2: *Structure of a scheme of work* (for one course unit)

It is beyond the competence of one person, for larger departments at least, to produce such a comprehensive document.

### A + B *Aims and Objectives*

Education's apparent obsession with these terms may seem tiresome. They are targets or goals which pose the question: *What do we want young people to achieve through this unit?* – enabling departments to check that their whole list of objectives is fulfilled by the sum of the units they teach.

Thinking about objectives is a vital safeguard against the scheme of work degenerating into a list of content, often prescribed by the examination board.

Objectives can be helpfully grouped into:

**1   Skills**

**2   Attitudes**

**3   Concepts**

**4   Knowledge**

**1   Skills**

The ability to perform tasks. These may in turn be grouped:

- communication
- study
- problem-solving
- creative and imaginative
- observation
- personal and social
- physical and practical
- numerical

**2   Attitudes**

The expression of values and personal qualities. Though definition is fraught with danger, the list below may be helpful:

- adaptability/flexibility
- commitment
- realism
- creativity
- curiosity
- reliability
- self-confidence
- empathy
- consideration for others
- honesty
- integrity
- self-discipline
- perseverance
- tolerance

**3   Concepts**

Generalisations which enable students to classify and organise knowledge, and to predict.

#### 4   Knowledge

Which is self-explanatory and coincident with content (see below)

Once objectives are set the question should be asked

- *How do we share the objectives with the students?*

### C   Content

Much content will be given by the National Curriculum and/or examination boards, but choice exists and so selection criteria are necessary. Is the proposed content

- up-to-date and appropriate to today's world;
- supportive of the department's whole programme – logically sequenced, avoiding overlap, building and reinforcing previous work;
- stimulating;
- appropriate to the age, intelligence and maturity of the students;
- within the constraints set by resources, examination boards and other bodies?

### D   Methods

Often omitted from schemes of work, but an absolutely vital stage if objectives are to mean anything at all.

A moment's reflection on the objectives for the unit, especially those in the skills and attitudes sections, will show that many can only be fulfilled by **how** the department teaches, rather that **what** it teaches. Adaptability, self-confidence, the ability to test hypotheses and to listen and speak effectively, for example, are content-free objectives.

Methodology forges the connection between content and objectives – by what teaching/learning methods do we most effectively make this content achieve these objectives?

- What methods would be most effective?
- Are they varied and lively, encouraging active participation on the part of students?
- Do they represent a coherent offering across a year, and a progression from year to year, rather than a 'firework display'?

### E   Resources

Include the human as well as the physical.

- Are we using the expertise of the teaching team most effectively? (Would, for example, a lead lesson by the team member with greatest expertise be helpful?)

- How can we most effectively use the service of the special needs department – to look at resources and work programmes for readability, advise on particular students or groups, co-teach with us etc.?
- What about the librarian?
- What about using people outside the department – from other departments or the community?
- Are the physical resources as far as possible
  - engaging and stimulating?
  - differentiated for the range of ability, offering opportunity for enrichment and extension for the more able, support and reinforcement for the less?
  - classified, stored and accessible to teachers and students?

## F    Evaluation

To keep it simple and supportive, evaluation can be divided conveniently into –

**1**    Student assessment

**What** is to be assessed is defined by the objectives for the unit and by the National Curriculum.

The questions to be answered are therefore

- By what methods do we most effectively ascertain that these objectives have been fulfilled? (Tests, end of unit assessment, group or homework exercises etc.?) How do we assess process objectives?
- How do the results of the assessment feed into the profiling system and therefore back to the students?
- What records should we and the students keep?

**2**    Evaluation of the unit

A team exercise, using data from pupil assessment, and other measures such as examination success, the take-up rate of the subject at option times, the enjoyment of teachers and students, students' comments (perhaps via profiles), and checks on written work. More sophisticated measures, such as classroom observation, shadowing a student, the use of other colleagues, other schools, advisers etc. are possible, and may be particularly useful to very small departments.

Evaluation should play both a formative and a summative role, enabling both adjustment of the programme as it goes along, and revision for next year.

The senior management team then suggested that there were five reasons for asking for a copy of the scheme:

- to ensure that such a document exists;

- to look for evidence of careful planning and clear layout;

- to see if what is in it affects daily practice and helps the teacher in her/his daily work;

- to form the basis of an agenda for departmental review;

- to bring together the work of several departments to see if coordination exists.

They then set their own agenda for reading schemes as follows:

## 1  Presentation

- Is the document well laid-out and word-processed in such a way that revision is straightforward?

- Do all department members, including part-timers, have copies?

- Is access easy to a newcomer?

## 2  Process

- Is there evidence of a process of collaborative writing or assembly, or is it a one-person document?

- Does any collaboration extend beyond the department into other departments or areas, and beyond the school into previous, parallel or succeeding schools/college, or the community?

## 3  Whole-school focus

- Does it consciously set out to interpret and build on the school aims?

- Does it take serious account of the work done in primary schools?

- Does it give high profile to whole- and cross-curricular elements such as numeracy, communication, PSE, environmental education . . .

- Does it make overt links with the work of other departments, making it clear who is responsible for what?

- Does it fulfil and take an active part in promoting whole-school policies towards equal opportunities of all kinds?

- Does it equally fulfil whole-school policies towards routines such as marking, assessment and recording, homework?

## 4  Content

- Is there a set of departmental objectives?

- Can clear links be seen between these objectives and the content?

- Is methodology given a high priority, as the link between content and objectives?

- Is there overt reference to continuity and progression into, through and out of courses?

- Does it give helpful suggestions on resources and indicate access to them?

## 5  Ethos

- Does an overall reading suggest the level of student involvement that the school believes in? Are objectives made clear to students? Is the process done for, with or to them?

Finally, the senior management team sought for ways to manage the writing of National Curriculum schemes of work. The central problem seemed to be the incremental nature of the curriculum. Science and other subjects need to have their schemes up and running, but at the same time need to coordinate content and cross-curricular themes with other subjects whose National Curriculum orders arrive much later. How was it possible to keep the schemes of work 'live'?

The senior management team decided on two strategies:

1   To reconstitute the department heads' meeting as an academic board (see Section C9), with the responsibility of *approving*, not just reading, all subject schemes of work. This process, akin to the role of an academic board in an institution of higher education, ensures that all department heads read the work of each department and, as far as possible, ensures they take a corporate view.

   This will imply a change in the nature of the business of heads of department meetings, and the senior management team will need to look at the implications of this for other agendas. Was some of it valuable, and who will mourn its passing?

2   To buy a big rubber stamp 'DRAFT' and a red ink pad for the school office, to be used on all schemes of work!

# D6
# Encouraging action research

**'Wedded to the curriculum and methodological developments'**

The above quotation from David Reynold's article 'Managing for improved school effectiveness: an international survey' underlines the fundamental issue for managers when they are seeking to manage change within schools. As any teacher knows, the most important attribute of successful teaching is the creation of opportunities that cause students to want to learn. An enormous investment in time and resources will have no effect unless the teacher exploits a variety of ways of engaging young minds.

In the same way, any investment in staff development courses that present preferred approaches to teaching and management will have little effect upon teachers unless these are embedded in their day-to-day experience. One of the most successful ways of encouraging development and change is the encouragement of **action research**. (It is worth noting that INSET funds may be used to release staff for action research.)

Action research is the business of involving teachers with school-based research which causes them to reflect on current practice and enact strategies for development and improvement. The added incentive to some action research is the link with higher education and the possibility of further professional accreditation. Such accreditation has a great appeal to teachers, since it is directly related to their everyday work and has an immediate pay-off.

Through staff appraisal it is possible for managers to identify those colleagues who might benefit themselves and the school through involvement with action research (C13). Not only will teachers develop their personal competencies, they may also encourage other colleagues to consider and adapt their approaches. In this way, the classroom teacher may perform an invaluable role as change agent within the school.

Long-term change will only take place where teachers feel convinced that there is a benefit for themselves and their students. Classroom practitioners are more likely to effect long-term change than managers, 'experts' or consultants.

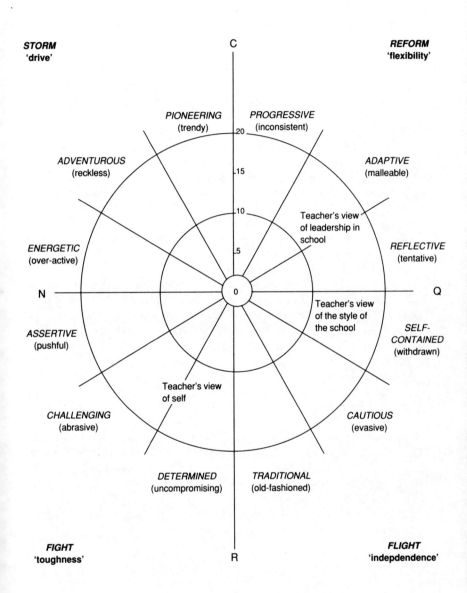

Figure 13   From *Helping Schools Change* by Harold Heller

## ■ First spot your change agent

One of the most useful instruments for gauging staff views of themselves and their school is Harold Heller's *Helping Schools Change*. Over three questionnaires, teachers are required to assess their attitudes to *self*, *school* and *leadership*. As a consequence, it is possible to place their attitudes within four described quadrants in respect of these three aspects of their professional life. The further positions are logged from the centre of the diagram, the more marked are the perceptions of the questionnaire's repondents. Readers are strongly recommended to refer to Harold Heller's very useful book to gain further information about the use of his instrument. Thus, in the example shown (Figure 13), the teacher sees *herself* with a marked tendency to be 'CHALLENGING', while she sees the *school* within which she works as having a tendency to be 'SELF-CONTAINED' and the style of *leadership* as 'ADAPTIVE'. In this case, it is clear that there is a tension within the individual and the possibility that she is frustrated in the school. Once the issues have been discussed, it may be discovered that there are aspects of school management which could be usefully examined by the teacher in question by way of action research. For example, she might offer much to the school if she were to mount an enquiry into 'The ways in which decisions are made in the school'. In any event, the effective manager will look to channel the energies of his/her potential change agent. If not, she may go elsewhere or feel frustrated and be a malign influence within the school.

At the same time it may be evident, through an appraisal or staff development interview, that another teacher is frustrated by the way he teaches students in groups. Through focused action research, he may be able to evaluate his performance and develop approaches and resources which lend themselves to more satisfactory management of teaching and learning. His analysis of current practice in his own and other lessons may lead to recommendations which have repercussions in all areas of the curriculum. In other words, his dissatisfaction with his own performance may lead to enhancement of performance across the curriculum.

An excellent example of Action Research in practice is Mike Hughes' *Flexible Learning in Practice*, Network Educational Press (1992).

# D7
# An agenda for self-review

The purpose of this section is to provide a checklist for review of the school's performance, and a means of following this through into detailed action plans for each area for development. Such a list can be used in a number of ways:

1   As an aide-memoire – jogging the memory that an area of school life has not been overhauled for many years. It may well be because the area is functioning perfectly well and is best left alone, but it may equally be that it has been neglected.

2   As a record of review over time, by recording dates, personnel or any other brief summary data against the heading.

3   As a basis for cyclic review of the main functions of the school. This is a demanding task, but may well be the approach favoured by some – over say a five year cycle (there seems little point in making it longer because of the pace of change), each faculty and year group, the major cross- and whole-curricular elements, and the main aspects of organisation are reviewed.

4   Use of the first four column headings in the table (Figure 14) enables a closer focus on the precise need. If homework has been registered as an area of concern, does that concern stem from

   • homework policy – have we one? Is it appropriate?

   • provision – do we set enough, too much, is the timetable right?

   • resources – do we have enough texts, worksheets, and is our resource centre good enough to facilitate stimulating homework?

   • quality – is it repetitive copying or completion, or is it stimulating?

5   When linked with the year planner, the checklist can be used to phase a scheme logically into the development plan. The compiling of a policy for health education in year 1 is followed by the implementation of provision and the necessary resources in year 2, and a review of the quality of what is going on in year 3.

| | POLICY | PROVISION | QUALITY | RESOURCES | Year 1 | Year 2 | Year 3 |
|---|---|---|---|---|---|---|---|
| *Whole curriculum* | | | | | | | |
| Aims | | | | | | | |
| Primary/secondary | | | | | | | |
| Sec/tertiary | | | | | | | |
| Key Stage 3 | | | | | | | |
| Key Stage 4 | | | | | | | |
| post-16 | | | | | | | |
| Library | | | | | | | |
| Resource centre | | | | | | | |
| Study skills | | | | | | | |
| Pastoral curriculum | | | | | | | |
| Assessment/marking | | | | | | | |
| Homework | | | | | | | |
| RoA/profiling | | | | | | | |
| Differentiation | | | | | | | |
| SEN | | | | | | | |
| Teaching and Learning | | | | | | | |
| Equal opps – | | | | | | | |
| gender | | | | | | | |
| multicultural | | | | | | | |
| disability | | | | | | | |
| | | | | | | | |
| *Cross-curriculum* | | | | | | | |
| IT | | | | | | | |
| EIU | | | | | | | |
| PSE | | | | | | | |
| Environmental ed | | | | | | | |

| | POLICY | PROVISION | QUALITY | RESOURCES | Year 1 | Year 2 | Year 3 |
|---|---|---|---|---|---|---|---|
| Health ed | | | | | | | |
| Careers ed | | | | | | | |
| European awareness | | | | | | | |
| *Subject curriculum* | | | | | | | |
| NC Core | | | | | | | |
| English | | | | | | | |
| Maths | | | | | | | |
| Science | | | | | | | |
| NC Foundation | | | | | | | |
| D & T | | | | | | | |
| Geography | | | | | | | |
| History | | | | | | | |
| Mod Languages | | | | | | | |
| Art | | | | | | | |
| Music | | | | | | | |
| PE | | | | | | | |
| RE | | | | | | | |
| Other subjects | | | | | | | |
| *Extended curriculum* | | | | | | | |
| Whole school | | | | | | | |
| Exam arrangements | | | | | | | |
| Results at 14+ | | | | | | | |
| 16+ | | | | | | | |
| 17 and 18+ | | | | | | | |
| PTR | | | | | | | |
| Contact ratio | | | | | | | |

| | POLICY | PROVISION | QUALITY | RESOURCES | Year 1 | Year 2 | Year 3 |
|---|---|---|---|---|---|---|---|
| *Management and staff* | | | | | | | |
| (Teaching & non-teaching) | | | | | | | |
| Structure | | | | | | | |
| Salary, allowances, merit pay | | | | | | | |
| Job descriptions | | | | | | | |
| Communication | | | | | | | |
| SMT | | | | | | | |
| Middle management | | | | | | | |
| HoDs | | | | | | | |
| Pastoral heads | | | | | | | |
| Form tutors | | | | | | | |
| Ancillary staff | | | | | | | |
| technicians | | | | | | | |
| librarians | | | | | | | |
| caretaking | | | | | | | |
| secretarial | | | | | | | |
| catering | | | | | | | |
| Staff duties | | | | | | | |
| Teaching/marking loads | | | | | | | |
| Timetable | | | | | | | |
| Cover arrangements | | | | | | | |
| Budget/finance management | | | | | | | |
| Finance monitoring | | | | | | | |
| | | | | | | | |
| *Staff development* | | | | | | | |
| Teaching staff | | | | | | | |
| Non-teaching staff | | | | | | | |

|  | POLICY | PROVISION | QUALITY | RESOURCES | Year 1 | Year 2 | Year 3 |
|---|---|---|---|---|---|---|---|
| Governors |  |  |  |  |  |  |  |
| Management development |  |  |  |  |  |  |  |
| Appraisal |  |  |  |  |  |  |  |
|  |  |  |  |  |  |  |  |
| *Environment* |  |  |  |  |  |  |  |
| H&S |  |  |  |  |  |  |  |
| Care and maintenance |  |  |  |  |  |  |  |
| Display |  |  |  |  |  |  |  |
| in classrooms |  |  |  |  |  |  |  |
| in circulation areas |  |  |  |  |  |  |  |
| outside |  |  |  |  |  |  |  |
| Pupils |  |  |  |  |  |  |  |
| Attendance |  |  |  |  |  |  |  |
| Rewards |  |  |  |  |  |  |  |
| Rules/behaviour |  |  |  |  |  |  |  |
| Dress |  |  |  |  |  |  |  |
| Expectations |  |  |  |  |  |  |  |
| Grouping |  |  |  |  |  |  |  |
| Records/reports |  |  |  |  |  |  |  |
| Pupil/pupil relations |  |  |  |  |  |  |  |
| Teacher/pupil relations |  |  |  |  |  |  |  |
|  |  |  |  |  |  |  |  |
| *Links beyond school* |  |  |  |  |  |  |  |
| Parents |  |  |  |  |  |  |  |
| Parental involvement |  |  |  |  |  |  |  |
| Support agencies |  |  |  |  |  |  |  |
| Media |  |  |  |  |  |  |  |

| | POLICY | PROVISION | QUALITY | RESOURCES | Year 1 | Year 2 | Year 3 |
|---|---|---|---|---|---|---|---|
| Governors | | | | | | | |
| Community | | | | | | | |
| Business community | | | | | | | |
| Other schools/colleges | | | | | | | |
| preceding | | | | | | | |
| parallel | | | | | | | |
| succeeding | | | | | | | |

Figure 14    School checklist

DEVELOPMENT PLAN FOR . . . . . . . . . . . . . . . .

STATEMENT OF AIM:

TO BE MANAGED BY:
INVOLVING (personnel):

IMPLEMENTATION PLAN (including timescale):

RESOURCE NEEDS:
i  Development Costs

ii  Running Costs

SUCCESS CRITERIA (and any other evaluation data):

Figure 15    Action plan

For each area where development is needed, a concise statement of intention is entered into the appropriate box – 'to introduce A level Russian', 'to raise the attendance rate by 5%', 'to redesign assessment policy and practice to take account of national tests at 14'. A justification could also be entered, if the box were redesigned – 'national priority', 'internal review', 'external inspection'.

Each of these having been entered on the year planner, a simple one-page plan is drawn up for carrying out each task, such as Figure 16 on page 149.

What follows is therefore an attempt at a classified list of most aspects of a school, from which many things are doubtless missing, but which contains enough to jog the memory. With it is the outline of a one-page plan for the carrying out of the required action in the chosen areas.

# D8
# Sample year planner

The number of processes and events which the school has to manage during the year, and the various groups who have to be involved in each, is so great that the drawing up of a calendar is essential. The outline (Figure 16) offers a draft format and some ideas to start the process off.

| | EXTERNAL EVENTS | SMT | GOVERNORS | ACADEMIC BOARD | STAFF MTGS | INSET DAYS |
|---|---|---|---|---|---|---|
| SEPTEMBER | new school year | exam results analysis appraisal begins | | dept annual reports to SMT | | |
| OCTOBER | destination stats arrive | assemble annual review data | summary of dept reports; and annual review data | appraisal begins discussions of report with SMT line manager | | |
| NOVEMBER | annual review | | | | | |
| DECEMBER | | redraft devt plan | | | | |
| JANUARY | form 7 | draft budget | consider draft budget | consider draft budget | | |
| FEBRUARY | budget confirmed | final budget organise departmental GRIDS survey | approve budget | | | |
| MARCH | | budgets to depts annual update of SDP | receive SDP | receive SDP | | |
| APRIL | new financial year | appraisal ends annual staff devt plan written | | appraisal ends | | |
| MAY | | timetable written headteacher appraisal begins | | | | |
| JUNE | f.y. outturn figs | | AGM | | | |
| JULY | | headteacher appraisal ends | | | | |
| AUGUST | exam results | | | | | |

Figure 16   Sample year planner

# Further Reading

Brighouse, *What Makes a Good School?*, Network Educational Press (1991)

Earley and Fletcher-Campbell, *The Time to Manage*, NFER-Nelson (1989)

Heller, *Helping Schools Change*, CSCS (1985)

Hughes, *Flexible Learning in Practice*, Network Educational Press (1992)

Reid, Holly and Hopkins, *Towards the Effective School*, Blackwell (1987)

Reynolds, *Managing for Improved School Effectiveness*, School Organisation Vol 9, No 2

*Reviewing School Departments*, SCDC/Longman (1989)

Spinks and Caldwell, *The Self-Managing School*, Falmer Press (1988)